SHAKESPEARE

ON LOVE AND FRIENDSHIP

SHAKESPEARE
ON LOVE AND FRIENDSHIP

Allan Bloom

The University of Chicago Press
Chicago and London

Shakespeare on Love and Friendship originally appeared as a part of *Love and Friendship* by Allan Bloom.

Until his death in 1992, Allan Bloom was codirector of the University of Chicago's John M. Olin Center for Inquiry into the Theory and Practice of Democracy and the John U. Nef Distinguished Service Professor in the Committee on Social Thought and in the College. His books include *The Closing of the American Mind* and (with Harry V. Jaffa) *Shakespeare's Politics* (published by the University of Chicago Press).

The University of Chicago Press, Chicago 60637
The University of Chicago Press, Ltd., London
Copyright © 1993, 2000 by the Estate of Allan Bloom
All rights reserved.
University of Chicago Press edition 2000
Printed in the United States of America

ISBN 0-226-06045-4

09 08 07 06 05 04 03 02 01 00   1 2 3 4 5

Library of Congress Cataloging-in-Publication Data

Bloom, Allan David, 1930–1992
    Shakespeare on love and friendship / Allan Bloom.
        p.   cm.
    Includes bibliographical references and index.
    Contents: Romeo and Juliet—Antony and Cleopatra—Measure for measure—Troilus and Cressida—The winter's tale—Hal and Falstaff.
    ISBN 0-226-06045-4 (paper: alk. paper)
        1. Shakespeare, William, 1564–1616—Criticism and interpretation.
2. Love in literature. 3. Friendship in literature. 4. Sex in literature.
5. Shakespeare, William, 1564–1616—Tragedies. 6. Shakespeare, William,
1564–1616—Tragicomedies. 7. Tragedy. 8. Tragicomedy. I. Title.

PR3069.L6 B58   2000
    822.3′3——dc21   99-055777

⊖ The paper used in this publication meets the minimum requirements of the American National Standard for Information Sciences—Permanence of Paper for Printed Library Materials, ANSI Z39.48–1992.

To Michael Z. Wu

CONTENTS

INTRODUCTION

Arnaldo Momigliano, the great historian of classical antiquity, once said to me that if Shakespeare had only become dominant before the beginning of the nineteenth century, we would have been spared Rousseau. I never asked him precisely what he meant, but I have always construed the remark to mean that to compensate for the human void left by the Enlightenment and its natural science, Shakespeare would have been a much healthier influence than Rousseau and the Romanticism he engendered. The Romantics had much to do with raising Shakespeare to the undisputed throne he now occupies, but their mediation tainted Shakespeare, and they were already themselves solidly established. Momigliano's remark appears right to me, for Shakespeare seems to be the mirror of nature and to present human beings just as they are. His poetry gives us the eyes to see what is there. The difference between Shakespeare and the Romantics is measured by the utter absence of didacticism in him. There is no intention in him to reconstruct the soul in order to make a place for human meaning, or to establish ideals in an ideal-less world, or to save the family and its relations from the corrosive of bourgeois rationalism. In short, Shakespeare has no project for the betterment or salvation of mankind. This does not mean that, in general, he did not believe that the truth would benefit men, but he did not think that the artist is defined as the man of responsibility. His plays remind us of the classical goal of contemplation rather than the modern aspiration to transform. Shakespeare did not consider himself the legislator of mankind. He faithfully records man's problems and does not evidently propose to solve them. It is not accurate to describe him as a genius or a creator.

He is too much immersed in the wonders of nature to focus on himself as the most important being in it. He does not try to create as did the Romantics; he tries to record nature.

Shakespeare's naturalness is what induces me to meditate on his plays in this discussion of human connectedness. I hope through doing so to articulate something of a premodern view of man's relations with his fellows, to provide serious, and perhaps more satisfactory, alternatives to our characteristic ways of looking at things. For example, Shakespeare's depiction of love does not require an elaborate psychology to explain the miracle of deep involvement, because he does not need to derive community from the premise of radical isolation and selfishness. He does not begin, as does Rousseau, from a Cartesian radical doubt and then try to put the machine back together again. He begins from the evidence that we are involved, presupposing that self and other are not in extreme opposition. Although natural science may teach us many useful things, Shakespeare does not presuppose that it is simply the privileged way of knowing or that it can dissolve the most powerful everyday experiences that men and women have. He preserves the phenomena, and analyzes the difficulties without an *a priori* framework that determines them. Human beings are connected and also disconnected, and the primacy of one over the other is not dictated by plausible postulates. Shakespeare's plays are full of the most beautiful conjunctions and the most brutal disjunctions, and it is an urgent necessity to find out how he saw all of this, because he is wise and because he does not share our common assumptions.

Shakespeare's naturalness is attested to by the strange fact that he is the only classical author who remains popular. The critical termites are massed and eating away at the foundations, trying to topple him. Whether they will succeed will be a test of his robustness. They want to teach us that he is the bastion of all the pernicious prejudices rather than our friend and liberator. But it is still true today that all over the world the titles of Shakespeare's plays have a meaning that speaks to common consciousness. *Hamlet, Lear, Othello* all call forth images in the minds of all classes of men across national boundaries. Perhaps the understanding of, or even acquaintance with, Shakespeare's plays is rather thin, but no one reacts with boredom or the sense that he stands only for bookish edification. This is why the theater is so lively in England and they keep producing such wonderful actors there. Racine and Molière in France, Lessing and Goethe in Germany, and Dante and Petrarch in Italy have no vitality in the eyes of ordinary young persons. They are dead, merely culture. No normal young person would prefer spending time with one of these great writers to going to a concert of the latest rock group. Shakespeare is practically our only link with the classic and the past. The future of education has much to do with whether we will be able to cling to him or not.

chapter one

ROMEO AND JULIET

Romeo and Juliet is always greeted by the young with immediate sympathy, somehow expressing the essence of love, what it ought to be, a permanent possibility, a fulfillment of every renascent hope and a thing to be admired. However far away this love affair may be from any real experience young men and women have today, however alien to the prevalent atmosphere of either careful and contractual relations or careless promiscuity, its two star-crossed lovers engage the admiration of most people without any need for instruction. Love at first sight, tapping the most generous sentiments and focusing the whole of two persons' energies on each other, bringing out the best in each, suppressing the petty and ugly passions, seems to be good manifestly and always possible. Here is a natural imperative. Students find Romantic novels artificial, full of prejudices, and infinitely distant from the way they approach sexual relations, but *Romeo and Juliet*, in a strange way, avoids all this. What Romantic novel could be used to legitimize the life of street gangs as *Romeo and Juliet* was in *West Side Story*? It transcends the quibbles about male and female roles while leaving behind the psychological complexities of attachment characteristic of Romantic novels. Shakespeare's women have a range and diversity that make us forget the constrained and constructed women of the Romantics. The total distinction between men and women and their roles is not present in Shakespeare, and women are capable of assuming male disguise in order to perform the male deeds that men are

All parenthetical citations in this chapter are to Shakespeare's *Romeo and Juliet*, ed. Brian Gibbons, Arden Edition (1980; rpt. London: Routledge, 1988).

frequently unable to perform for themselves. Shakespeare is never a
sucker for theory, and this communicates itself to his audiences.

Love is very much Shakespeare's theme, and in reflecting on love
in Shakespeare one must begin with *Romeo and Juliet*, for it appears to
be the purest description of the phenomenon of love and depiction of
its fate in the world. Shakespeare is a middle ground between the ancient poets whose tragedies hardly spoke of love and the Romantic poets whose sad tales concerned only love. Serious writers in antiquity,
with the strange exception of Plato, did not present men and women
in love as the most serious of beings facing the most serious of problems. The reasons for this should be investigated further, but we may
say that it has something to do with the primacy of virtue and reason
over the passions in the classical view, whereas the Romantics made
love their theme precisely because of their preference for the passions
over virtue and reason. Christian Europe, of course, has an ambiva-
lent and ambiguous history so far as love goes, but certainly the official
position depreciates erotic love in favor of Christian love or *agapē*.
This is a question that interests Shakespeare greatly.

Two of his tragedies are about couples in love, as their very titles indicate, *Romeo and Juliet* and *Antony and Cleopatra*, while *Troilus and
Cressida*, if not a tragedy, approaches that status. They are the only
plays that have two names in their titles, indicating that shared tragic
fates belong above all to lovers. There are no authentic love affairs in
the history plays, where politics, seemingly unerotic, is the primary
theme. The comedies, of course, are shot through with sexual themes.
And this is perfectly classical, treating man's eroticism as one of the
things that make him ridiculous, the angle from which the disproportion between his aspirations and his reality is most evident. The ancients may have relegated love to comedy for reasons of edification,
not wanting very ordinary human beings to be encouraged in passions
that are most often empty, or for more philosophic reasons, holding
that man's dependency on his body and his being duped by illusions
are what love is all about. Shakespeare's tragedies are less tragic than
those of Aeschylus and Sophocles, and his comedies less comic than
those of Aristophanes. The ancients were either all tragedy or all
comedy; Socrates at the end of his great discussion about love in the
Symposium argues against the tragedian Agathon and the comedian
Aristophanes and reproaches them for not being able to mix the gen-
res. Shakespeare relaxes the twin tensions that end in either tears or

laughter, taking tragedy a bit less seriously and comedy a bit more seriously than did the ancients. And, just as in Plato, love makes its way onto the scene between high political gravity and low sexual levity. Love appears to be a link between the high and low in man, and Shakespeare devotes much of his talent to looking into this. Love is surely not the whole meaning of life for Shakespeare, but it just as surely flatters some of man's dearest aspirations. What could be more wonderful than uniting one's most intense pleasure with the highest activity and the most noble and beautiful deeds and words? Such is the promise of love.

Romeo and Juliet are the perfect pair of lovers. They are beautiful, they are young, they are noble, and they are rich. People get angry about lookism, ageism, elitism, and so on, but, when it comes to Romeo and Juliet, I find that outrage is disarmed, and most everybody becomes a partisan of these youngsters. With envy silenced, even the most sparingly endowed of us gets satisfaction from this love, thus proving that you do not have to make the world ugly in order to compensate us for our defects. Man naturally craves a perfection that he cannot attain. But at least part of that perfection consists in our capacity to conceive it. The greatest writers satisfy this craving, at least for the moment, and thus make us momentarily perfect. Misguided resentment can attempt to destroy the models of perfection in order to balm the wounds of the disadvantaged, but in so doing it deprives all of us of our most natural pleasure. When reading the beautiful words in their love scenes, only the most perverse person would throw the book aside because it hurts too much to think that one will never have anything quite so good. Rather, the natural inclination seems to be, for a moment, to identify and to enhance one's lesser sentiments by the grander ones Shakespeare lays out for us. "This is what I felt but did not have the words to say" is what the healthy reader thinks. Leveling literature and literary theory would deprive us of what is perhaps the dearest longing of our natures, one which Shakespeare satisfies so fully for us.

The crushing of these two winning beings seems the least inevitable ending among Shakespeare's tragedies, the product of mere chance. In other plays, our first rebellion against the fall of a great person is followed by a sad and wise recognition that this end is in the nature of things, residing in the character of the person. Macbeth's ambition leads him ineluctably to crime and death, but Romeo kills himself only because he believes that Juliet is dead. How does that difference between appearance and reality follow necessarily from the lover's nature? This is the mystery of the play. It can appear to be melodrama rather than tragedy. *Romeo and Juliet,* no matter how many times read or seen, always induces a reaction that if this or that little thing had been changed, they would have lived happily ever after. There seems to be no reason why this great tragedy could not have been replaced by the lesser tragedy of their settling down together, watching their beauties disappear slowly with age while they became bored with each other.

In speculating about the tragedy's denouement, one is forced to the conclusion that it has something to do with the problem of family. The names of the Capulet and Montague families are almost as well known as those of Romeo and Juliet. The authority, or even tyranny, of parents induces the classic conflict between inclination and duty, and the love affair between Romeo and Juliet flies in the face of what are at least conventionally understood to be duties. The problem of squaring nature with convention is a suitable theme for drama. The family, which has its roots in erotic necessities, is profoundly anti-erotic. It surrounds young people with all kinds of noes, and, in the grand tradition of the family, it uses sexual alliances for the sake of property, status, and political arrangements.

Romeo and Juliet never have any doubt about the superiority of their love to any commandment that might prohibit it, and Shakespeare presents them in such a way that the audience will have no doubts either about that superiority. This pair represents the natural rights of love. Romeo's side of it is hardly illustrated in the play, but he is fully aware that his love is not a thing his parents would have approved of. And the innocent child, Juliet, proves to be a natural at deception, unhesitatingly lying and misleading her parents. Shakespeare does not argue for the dignity of the family; everyone is meant to side unqualifiedly with the lovers. "All the world loves a lover." The parents are coarse, selfish, and unfeeling. The mother can speak only incoherent platitudes in recommending to Juliet the husband who has been chosen for her. But with his sympathies wholly on the side of love, Shakespeare perhaps wishes to teach us that it, like all idealisms, must come to terms with familial, religious, and political demands. Romeo and Juliet never think of just running away together and living off love, perhaps because everywhere there are conventions.

Love in Shakespeare knows no bounds of propriety, whether laid down by family or country. It has a natural cosmopolitanism. The immediate love of the beautiful is beyond the limits of loyalty, limits that are generally easily accepted where the erotic love of the beautiful does not come into conflict with them. Even in the critical moment when Juliet learns that her cousin, Tybalt, representing her family, has been killed by her husband, she has only a moment of hesitation before returning even more furiously to her faith while becoming indifferent to her cousin's death. This would appear to all of us to be fanaticism if it were not for love, the fanaticism we all adore. Treachery of every other kind seems merely despicable, and it is a great tribute to love that it can provide a passport, recognized by so many, for travel beyond the boundaries. But the loyalists have their day too.

In *Romeo and Juliet,* there is a political problem typical of Renaissance Italy, which is also the seat of modern love in Shakespeare's writings. Machiavelli, a writer whom I am persuaded Shakespeare knew very well, speaks of the family quarrels that racked the independent cities of Italy, quarrels exploited by tyrants and potential tyrants and often connected with political and religious factions. This problem is representative of the more generic question of faction, of which all modern political thinkers, including Shakespeare, were keenly aware. According to the ancient political philosophers, the cities could be founded only when they had enough power to suppress the unlimited powers of the fathers. The blood tie, which forms the clan, must be suppressed, often violently. In Italy, the code of the clan reasserted itself as a result of the feebleness of the political rulers. The too gentle or merciful character of the princes is what Machiavelli blames and Shakespeare depicts. The Prince himself recognizes that he has been too weak, but never acts strongly until it is too late, if one can consider even the end of the play as a real reassertion of his power. He says, in a thought that accords perfectly with Machiavelli's teaching,[1] that "Mercy but murders, pardoning those that kill" (III.i.199). But he appears not to have been able to act upon this thought. The difficulty is less any lack of brute force than a spiritual weakness, an infection apparently stemming from the attraction of mercifulness. This does not mean that in a less corrupt political order, Romeo and Juliet would not have had to overcome parental resistance, but their problem would not have been rendered tragic by civil war. Friar Laurence tries to use this pair of rare and beautiful love birds as the means of restoring civil peace. But only their destruction permits the peace of death to descend over the two families, whose only heirs disappear. This tells us much about the relationship of love and politics.

Romeo is the prototype of the Romantic lover and poet in his perpetual longing and his concern for things that the rest of men are too sunk in the mud of daily life to care about; in his moodiness and despair about the fragility of the golden links that bind him to his beloved; in his simultaneous melancholy and enthusiasm. But he is not a Romantic hero because Shakespeare does not permit him to dominate the stage, and although he is sympathetically portrayed, in the whole of Shakespeare's works and even in this play there are many other types that can rival and surpass Romeo. He has a ridiculous side that is properly ridiculed, and that is lacking in a Saint-Preux or a Werther. He is passion without reflection or calculation, and although such passion is rare and attractive, Shakespeare makes it appear to be a thing of youth without making youth appear to be the best age. Romeo is absolutely unqualified in his feelings and in his expressions of them. He is determined and intractable. Neither his enemies nor his friends can have any effect on his behavior, which means that he is an unusually ineffective manager of the conspiracy that would be necessary to bring his plans to a successful conclusion. He thinks that love is sufficient unto itself, self-justifying, and that it has to make no compromises with men or gods. He is a bit of a bore and a pest for his friends and associates because his attention is elsewhere, preoccupied with his hopelessness or his hopefulness, living in a different and higher world than they do. He exists only for the delicious moments of perfect understanding between Juliet and himself. Whatever justification Shakespeare provides for Romeo is in three scenes: their first encounter, the avowal of love in the garden, and the end of the one night they spend together. This last, by the way, may be Romeo's only completed experience of sexual love, as it is certainly Juliet's.

Critics have disputed whether it is a strength or a weakness in Romeo's character that is depicted in the opening scenes of the play, where he is totally and desperately in love with Rosaline (also linked to the Capulet family, which seems to have the only good girls in town) and then he changes his eternal love in an instant. This makes one wonder, if he had lived and Juliet had not, whether he would not have found others. He is certainly in love with love and believes, as lovers must, that the object of his love is unique in the world and that no other could be loved in her place. It is not enough to say that Juliet, unlike Rosaline, is ready to reciprocate. This would mean that Romeo's love would be willing to compromise on the principle of availability. Certainly love, as Romeo understands it, must be reciprocal, unlike the love directed to a god or a goddess. Yet love for him is a religion, "the devout religion of mine eye" (I.ii.90). And if the eyes were to see another more beautiful, they would be "transparent heretics" (I.ii.93). He rejects Benvolio's reasonable suggestion that he make comparisons and then choose, on the grounds that this would be contrary to his religious faith. "I'll go along, no such sight to be shown, / But to rejoice in splendour of mine own" (I.ii.102–103). He understands love as a product of opposites, like the world itself: "O anything of nothing first create" (I.i.175). His imagery includes pagan and Christian elements.

Does Romeo's initial love for Rosaline portray a man with a natural talent for love just going through his apprenticeship before entering on his vocation? Or does it mean that the whole apparatus of love depends on shifting opinions and mere imagination? Certainly, and this is explicit both in the comments of others and in Romeo's own self-awareness, imagination is his faculty. The vexed question of the desirability and reliability of imagination is raised by this character. In his happy moments, he can beautify the world with the images Shakespeare lends him, but when his lover's imagination fails, he imagines only death, oblivious to or contemptuous of whatever charms reality might offer.

Love is a very strange thing, this powerful desire to be together with another that gets in the way of life's serious activities, such as providing for one's preservation or governing men and nations. It creates an almost unbearable dualism in life unless, by giving oneself to it completely and forgetting the rest, one unifies life. This kind of unity in pleasure and high aspiration is one of man's most flattering hopes. Love is a substitute for the comparatively burdensome and dull practice of the virtues, because it at least seems to substitute for those virtues. A lover is courageous, generous, and beyond the quibbles of mere justice. He is proof against the petty and corrosive desires and passions. He is, of course, not characterized by the less attractive virtues, moderation and wisdom. Romeo is surely bold and willing to risk his life; there is plenty of evidence for that in the play. When he is in his right mind, he is intelligent and clever, as one sees when he is the only one able to keep up with Mercutio. He has friends, like Benvolio and Mercutio, who are clearly decent men. Romeo has no marked virtues, in any strict sense of the word, but he has generous dispositions, and love can turn them into persuasive simulacra of virtue. He might have been a warrior, except that the love of the beautiful predominates over any ambition he might have had. His easy victory over Tybalt shows what kind of a fighter he must have been, but his joys are not those of honor or vengeance or even conquest, except of his beautiful beloved. His virtues and vices are all summed up in the fact of his suicide at the only apparent death of Juliet. He is a perfect youth. We can recognize this only too well when he tells Friar Laurence that nobody as old as that worthy priest could understand his situation. He is all enthusiasm, imagination, and faith, without any appreciation of the sobriety of age.

Juliet's qualities are without the ambiguities present in Romeo. Beauty as the promise of virtue is fulfilled. She has experienced no love before Romeo and was already resisting promising her parents to love the lover they would foist upon her. There is no hesitation from the first moment she exchanges a word with Romeo. Romeo is her life. She is perfectly feminine, but Shakespeare puts her beyond the ordinary demands of modesty. She knows she should say no, but does not. Her assurance of her affections and her belief in what his form promises about his substance are such that she must show herself naked and unprotected to him. She tells him that she could make a show of modesty and reserve, but that she will only remind him that if he is merely a seducer, he will have used her ill. Here her femininity marvelously reminds of the necessity of modesty while dispensing with it. The intensity of her faith takes its place. This is ever so much higher than the games of love practiced by the French. For Juliet, there is neither low nor high in erotic matters, and we are relieved as much by the absence of the high as by that of the low. No love could be more perfect than her innocent eroticism. This child can make the act of love seem to be above all taint of sin. She waits impatiently for her first night with a man, full of bodily longing, faced squarely as such, but understood in such a way as to make that longing and its satisfaction a pure expression of all that seems best. Night will be the day of her love: "Hood my unmann'd blood, bating in my cheeks, / With thy black mantle, till strange love grow bold, / Think true love acted simple modesty" (III.ii.14–16). Never has bodily love had such noble and untarnished expression. Perhaps she represents what Rousseau prescribed in his attempt to reunify man after original sin split him, but it is only Shakespeare who can fill that prescription.

Yet this marvelous creature is treated with astounding brutality by the plot. Her sufferings much surpass those of Romeo. Her isolation in love is much more extreme than his. He is surrounded by friends. His family does not play a role and probably would not have been so fiercely opposed to accepting her among the Montagues, whereas the Capulets would not have gained a son but lost a daughter. Friar Laurence is much more the confidant of Romeo than of Juliet. Juliet has only the support of her nurse, not quite a valid interlocutor, who abandons her at the most terrible time. She has to confront Romeo's killing her beloved cousin and the fury of her parents. And above all, she is the one who has to appear to die and to wake up in the horrors of the grave. She has a moment of doubt when she learns of Tybalt's death and a moment of hesitation before she drinks the potion, but her recovery is so swift and so firm that those moments only serve to heighten her resoluteness.

The relationship between Romeo and Juliet is as powerful and unconditional as human relationships ever are, but when one reflects on it, the substance of their connection remains mysterious. Perhaps this is the mystery of love altogether, but our familiarity with the idea does not reduce its mysteriousness. Love has the advantage over other types of attachment, particularly those connected with family and country, that it does not appear to depend merely on accidents like blood (as is particularly underlined in this play), and that it requires none of the constraints of convention, duty, or law. It is free in every sense. All that one does in it one does with pleasure and enthusiasm. It is one's own, without constraint, although we are not the masters of our falling in or out of love. It is comparable on all these counts only to friendship of the higher kind described by Aristotle. Friendship, however, is a much calmer thing and can give a better account of itself inasmuch as one chooses a friend for his proved virtue. Friendship is a consequence of deliberate choice, whereas love is a kind of possession that requires so much faith, accompanied by a spectacular apprehension of the beautiful. A friend is good, while a beloved is beautiful. The beautiful has it all over the good in attractiveness. The appeal of the good is rational, that of the beautiful is passionate. Friendship is human, while love is divine.

In my own enthusiasm for Shakespeare I can only say that there is no better depiction of all of these qualities of love than in *Romeo and Juliet*. And there is also no better depiction of the strange mating of love and death. This play literally culminates in the tomb. From the outset, Romeo is filled with forebodings of death, and as Juliet bids farewell to him after their night together, she says, "Methinks I see thee, now thou art so low, / As one dead in the bottom of a tomb" (III.v.55–56). She divines here the denouement, which is probably the most horrible scene of death in all of Shakespeare, a writer who does not spare his audiences the sight of death. Juliet, in her terror as she drinks the potion, imagines not only the fearsome sight of death she will encounter, but also all of the human baggage of guilt and dread that accompanies it. The illusion of eternal life and beauty, the delicious, fleshy bodies that embrace and will never decay, is the opposite of the skeletons in the tomb. Shakespeare's joining of the two in this play is what is most shocking about it, the contrast between the hopes of love and the reality of death. Perhaps he is teaching us that the eros for the beautiful is the hopeless attempt to overcome the ugliness of the grave, an attempt of the unwise to adorn a very questionable world.

These two young persons, so admirably equipped for love but so innocent of the world, are sent out into it. We can begin to respond to the question of the inevitability of the tragic ending that seems so undeserved, by saying they are bound to collide with the city. The city with its laws has its own special ways of coping with death or avoiding it (particularly in preserving, by way of the family, the eternity of generations rather than of individuals). The lovers are not the Greek gods of whom we are so beautifully reminded by Greek statues, who are always young and beautiful. The charm of Romeo and Juliet is in their consideration only of the present, which they understand to be there always. But just as powerfully, we know that they are not merely unwise but haters of wisdom:

FRIAR: I'll give thee armour to keep off that word,
   Adversity's sweet milk, philosophy,
   To comfort thee though thou art banished.
ROMEO: Yet "banished"? Hang up philosophy.

> Unless philosophy can make a Juliet,
> Displant a town, reverse a Prince's doom,
> It helps not, it prevails not. Talk no more.
> FRIAR: O, then I see that mad men have no ears.
> ROMEO: How should they when that wise men have no eyes?
> FRIAR: Let me dispute with thee of thy estate.
> ROMEO: Thou canst not speak of that thou dost not feel.
> (III.iii.54–64)

If philosophy, as Shakespeare knew that Socrates had said, is learning how to die, then Romeo is not avid of that science. Youngsters are not supposed to be, but this is why youngsters must be supervised.

Thus wisdom's superiority, which none of the other characters illustrate, is restored by the message of the play as a whole. Shakespeare flatters our hopes and then smashes them. The sober teachings of moderation are given their due by the results of the charming immoderation Shakespeare appears to celebrate in the early parts of the play. The terrible consequences of their love could have been avoided at many points if either lover had been moderate or reflective, but this would have been like cutting the wings of birds and still expecting them to fly.

The problem of the play is that there is, with the possible exception of Mercutio, no figure of sufficient weight to counter the charm of love. In the opposition between Romeo and Friar Laurence, it is Romeo who always carries the day, both in the outcome of the plot and in moving the audience. If moderation is merely consolation when one's immoderate schemes fail, it is hardly choiceworthy. In the struggle between age and youth on the stage the preference almost always goes to youth, and wisdom inevitably is an attribute of age while love is one of the two or three primary attributes of hotheaded youth. One does not go to the theater to be taught compromises, however inevitable, between realism and idealism. Unless there are possible splendid representations of wise moderation, in the theater there is a simply tragic choice between the noble or beautiful and life. The choice of life is the coward's part and is never attractive to audiences. So it is represented even by Homer, when the shade of Achilles tells us that now, when he is in a position to survey the alternatives, he would prefer to be a serf on earth than to be the king of all the shades in Hades.[2] If he had acted on that conviction during his life, there would have been no *Iliad*.

To show that these are Shakespeare's own reflections and not merely my own, a glance at *The Tempest* is required. Critics, notably Coleridge, have remarked that Ferdinand and Miranda in *The Tempest* are very much like Romeo and Juliet. The suddenness and intensity of their love, as well as their innocence and good character, are alike. They are also from families at war, the king of Naples, Ferdinand's father, having been part of the plot to unseat the duke of Milan, Miranda's father. Their love has exactly the same potential for tragedy as does that of Romeo and Juliet. But that potential is prevented from being realized by the presence, *per impossibile,* of a genuinely wise man, the sort that would never be present in any real situation. Prospero, who has arranged this affair and brought the young people together, vigilantly supervises their relationship and fulfills a serious political project with their marriage. With Prospero, Shakespeare undertakes *the* most difficult problem for a dramatist, the presentation of a wise man, without making him into a buffoon, a knave, and most and worst of all, a bore. Art's near incapacity to make wisdom attractive was a problem addressed by both Plato and Rousseau.[3] The Platonic dialogues are one kind of partial resolution of this problem. Shakespeare proceeds by presenting him as a magician, a figure always appealing to popular audiences. The Savoyard Vicar may say, "I am happy," but even the mature Rousseau does not seem to believe it, and certainly Rousseau presents himself with an entirely different allure. But Prospero, whose very name means happiness, can, once one has removed a bit of glitter from kings and lovers, stake a claim to being a truly dramatic and appealing wise man. In a sense, *Romeo and Juliet,* as well as several other plays, can be seen to pose problems or conflicts that cannot be resolved in practice but with which a Prospero could in principle deal. Total preoccupation with the agony of the tragic heroes makes us think that there is an absolute impossibility of uniting nobility and happiness. But Prospero, by his person and by the deeds he performs, projects a half light onto the tragic scene that reminds us that life as such may not be tragic.

Miranda, as indicated by her very name, arouses that most specifically human reaction, wonder, which Aristotle tells us leads to either myth or philosophy.[4] Between Ferdinand and Miranda themselves it is all myth, that is, imagination and love. But the philosopher Prospero manages the myth for the sake of a reasonable outcome. "Oh, brave new world." This is what Miranda experiences, but Prospero is fully aware of what villains and clowns really populate this world. He makes Ferdinand pass love tests and actively tames his rebelliousness with punishments. He can prevent their consummation prior to marriage. He imposes an iron law of necessity on them that will protect them from the imprudence which on their own they would almost certainly commit. He delights in their beauty and their mutual attraction, things that he is too old to have any longer. But regret is not what he feels. He sees that they are fond and foolish. His satisfaction comes from his contemplation of them and their fulfilling of his plan. His daughter, from having been the isolated offspring of a failed duke of Milan, will be the queen of Naples, and her union with Ferdinand will make him into a generous and just king. They will love, and the fruits of their love will be useful to mankind.

The Tempest is a play about motives and motivations. Its lowest characters, Stephano, Trinculo, and Caliban, are creatures of bodily pleasure who can be rendered tolerable in the civil order only by bodily pinches and cramps. The layer above them is inhabited by Italian princes, Antonio, Sebastian, and Alonso, who practice ugly deeds for the sake of acquiring and maintaining rule. They are the princes described by Machiavelli, and for them Prospero prescribes imaginary terrors that produce bad conscience. But they are more human than the inhabitants of the psychological basement, because they, capable of doing more harm, are motivated by a certain spirituality, albeit a dark spirituality. The top floor of the social and political world is occupied by the two lovers, who are also motivated by imagination, but of the beautiful, thus dismissing the base, the petty, and the merely powerful from their vision. They are not wise, but the noble view of things will substitute, if imperfectly, for wisdom, which never truly rules in real states. Prospero with this couple solves the problem of his own succession, and he has channeled the illusions of love to the public benefit. He himself is beyond this house, which he has built and put in order, and above which he floats. Here we have *Romeo and Juliet* without tragedy, a Romeo and Juliet to whom we prefer Prospero. This is perhaps Shakespeare's greatest *tour de force*. Tragedy is prevented by Prospero. We must never forget that the potential of tragedy is here, but we must also never forget that there is something beyond tragedy. Prospero says that he will "retire me to my Milan, where / Every third thought shall be my grave."[5] This is about the right proportion and is the calm statement of a man who knows how to die, very different from the frantic oscillation between love and the tomb.

The last two persons in *Romeo and Juliet* who are important to our investigation are Mercutio and Friar Laurence. As soon as one mentions Mercutio's name, one thinks of the problem of obscenity in Shakespeare. A large proportion of Mercutio's lines are devoted to exquisite and witty dirty remarks and allusions. Shakespeare forces us to exercise our imagination in trying to figure out what Mercutio alludes to, and we are already stained by that activity. The commentators remain largely silent about these passages, I suppose because they regard them as comic relief and not part of the serious business of the tragedy, as if comic relief did not require as much explanation as any other aspect of a drama. Why does Shakespeare require comic relief when Sophocles does not? One can answer that he is trying to amuse the audience. But that would imply that so great an artist panders to the public at the expense of the integrity of his work. Maybe. But it should not be assumed that this is so, particularly since it can easily be an excuse for our laziness. Interpreters such as Eric Partridge can be of help, but he is far from being complete, and he postures so much in his role as a freethinker and sexually healthy man in England at mid-century that he himself becomes ridiculous and of doubtful reliability.[6]

Our first observation must simply be that the only character of a human weight perhaps equal to that of the principals has what we would call a foul mouth, which implies a foul mind to go with it. He is a real friend to Romeo, whom he dominates by powerful intelligence. He is also a spirited man, always ready for a fight. His obscenity is largely used in the service of his moonstruck friend, whom he tries to liberate from his attachment to Rosaline by means of ridicule. Of course, like everyone else in the play except for Friar Laurence and Juliet's nurse, he is unaware of Romeo's involvement with Juliet. Therefore his ignorance causes this healer of lovesickness to misdiagnose the case. But his intention is clearly good, although his ignorance contributes to the disaster. He might be said to be responsible for the tragedy by his confronting and provoking the enraged Tybalt, but he does so in order to protect Romeo. It is Romeo's attempt at peacemaking, his lover's vain hope to produce goodwill among men, that results in Mercutio's death. Thus Romeo must fight and kill Tybalt with the consequence that he is banished from Verona. Moreover, he believes the Capulet family will now be absolutely intractable. With Mercutio's death, Romeo loses a close friend who would have been an advisor and a protector. After Mercutio disappears from the scene, all good humor, wit, and obscenity disappear with him. From then on, Romeo is isolated and the atmosphere becomes very grim.

The elements in Mercutio's character are well mixed. He, like Tybalt, is extremely spirited, as Aristotle says friends must be,[7] but he is not eaten up by Tybalt's doglike rage. While not sharing Romeo's uncontrolled imagination and overgreat tenderness, he has a splendid poetic imagination, as is manifest in the Queen Mab speech, a real beauty about fantasy and vanity. And this noble poetic figure is one of the most obscene of Shakespeare's characters. It has been said that the Greeks didn't like to talk about eating or sex because both were signs of man's unfreedom. Something of this view of sex is brought to *Romeo and Juliet* by Mercutio, who is forgotten by everybody, including the audience, during the last three acts when he is no longer present. But to grasp the meaning of the play, we must remember him and the question mark he puts after the seductive sentiments of the lovers. His importance is underlined by the fact that his role in the play is entirely invented, independent of the sources Shakespeare used for it. Such invented characters are of decisive importance in carrying Shakespeare's message, as are Falstaff in the history plays and Enobarbus in *Antony and Cleopatra*. This play is about love, and love is related to obscenity by their common source in eroticism. But love and obscenity are at tension with each other, if not mutually exclusive. Juliet is never obscene, and Romeo is so only in his brilliant exchanges with Mercutio, which prove that when he is himself he is Mercutio's equal in wit and hence his worthy friend. Love and anger have in common that one does not joke about their objects, and if one does, the passions are either doused or are transformed into something else. Both love and anger require belief, and laughter liberates from belief. Only Romeo and Juliet love in the play, and all the others, with the exception of Friar Laurence, are in one way or another obscene.

One tends to forget just how obscene the first two acts of *Romeo and Juliet* are. Romeo and Juliet are surrounded by persons who talk most explicitly and unromantically about sex. The very first scene gives us a picture of lower-class male manners and morals. The servants of the Montague house chatter about their quarrel with the Capulets and the impending battle:

SAMPSON: I will show myself a tyrant: when I have fought with the
  men, I will be civil with the maids, I will cut off their heads.
GREGORY: The heads of the maids?
SAMPSON: Ay, the heads of the maids, or their maidenheads; take it in
  what sense thou wilt.
GREGORY: They must take it in sense that feel it.
SAMPSON: Me they shall feel while I am able to stand, and 'tis known
  I am a pretty piece of flesh.
GREGORY: 'Tis well thou art not fish; if thou hadst, thou hadst been
  Poor John. Draw thy tool—here comes of the house of
  Montagues.
SAMPSON: My naked weapon is out . . . (I.i.20–32)

These false tough guys mix the size and force of their organs into their battle talk. Similarly, in Act I, scene iii, the Nurse, who is permitted to participate in the formal announcement to Juliet that Paris has been chosen to be her groom, cannot help repeating several times over, in the presence of the innocent Juliet, her husband's stupid joke about how Juliet when she was a baby fell on her face but how she will, at an age of improved wit, fall on her back. This seems to her so hilarious and such an appropriate description of the human condition. She completes a perfect pair with Lady Capulet, who stiffly and hypocritically describes the appropriateness and beauty of the match proposed for Juliet. The lower class constitutes a background of the barnyard, a mixture of boasting and explicitness with sly allusions to the mentionable unmentionable. Their behavior seems to be perfectly acceptable in these good families. Perhaps this is because no aristocrat would think of imitating or being influenced by a servant any more than Mme. Duchâtelet was embarrassed to appear naked before her menservants.[8] Clearly, in Shakespeare's world it was not thought that the plant of high eroticism was so frail as to be unable to resist debunking by the brutish couplings of those without any refinement of soul. Love is not simply a construct or a diversion of energy from low to high. Romeo and Juliet are peculiarly invulnerable to this kind of influence, perhaps to their detriment. But Mercutio, who shares the earthy sexual awareness of the inferior persons, translates it to the highest level.

He is aware of how our most intense feelings indicate our comic dependence on "pretty pieces of flesh."

Obscenity changes love's transcendence into a fascination with the bodily needs and effects of eroticism. Somehow the disproportion between what we think love should be and what we actually are is laughable. So much of comedy turns on the unmasking of boasting, beginning from the pompous ass who slips on a banana peel and comes back to the level, or beneath it, of ordinary humanity, all the way to the highest claims of love of justice and love of God. We laugh because we are released from pieties in which we cannot entirely believe. This release may be a satisfaction because it allows our natures to go about their business without constantly measuring themselves against our pieties. But our need to laugh, the spirit of comedy, is as mysterious as our need to cry, the spirit of tragedy. Shakespeare never lets us give ourselves completely to either one of these two temptations.

If we follow Leo Strauss's division of Aristophanes' comedy into four kinds, blasphemy, slander, parody, and obscenity, then we must say that in Shakespeare, obscenity predominates. Blasphemy undermines belief in the gods, slander attacks the rulers of the city, parody mocks the tragic poets, and obscenity goes to the root of the family.[9] Obscenity is the gentlest of the four, and is not an utterly useless thing if man needs to take some critical stance toward the myths of the family and the erotic desires that lead us to the family. Surely obscenity is low, but it is not always the lowest or least interesting of Shakespeare's characters who are obscene, as is shown by the example of Falstaff.

Rousseau says that the French are so indescribably filthy-minded that their language is necessarily pure, a sentiment echoed by Goethe.[10] Rousseau says that an unashamed directness is not shameless and that men and women in simpler societies were the masters of such speech, and his Romantic followers made some attempt to enrich the language of eros while recovering its spirit. This, as so much else that stems from Rousseau, had the character of a project, and it sat uneasily with the highness of love and women he promoted. But it does not do simply to say that men were more able to talk about the facts of life in Shakespeare's England than they were in the nineteenth century and everywhere in the West until only yesterday. Shakespeare was able to choose what he wanted from his own times and mold it to his purposes.

   Shakespeare's obscenity is peculiarly worthy of our study, because
it can help us recognize our incapacity to talk well about certain matters that are very important for our lives. Today dirty talk is routine
and meaningless, and, at the same time, the structures of the sacred in
love and the family have been dismantled in such a way as to render the
point of Shakespeare's humor almost meaningless. The use of the
word "fuck" at all times and in all contexts today is not primarily a sign
of liberation or willingness to face facts. It certainly does indicate a re-
cent change in the way of looking at things that has complex causes,
but the upshot is a radical impoverishment of speech and, corre-
spondingly, of thought and desire. Our use of explicitly sexual language permits two debasements: meaningless and costless sex and
also an "objectification" of sex and its manipulation by science, natural or social, for unerotic purposes. Our own "post-Romantic" mode
of speech about these matters is inextricably bound up with the attempt to produce a science of sex, which requires an embarrassingly
inadequate technical terminology to make it easier for doctors to
speak the unspeakable. This both replaces love talk and leads to a simplification and cleaning up of obscenity. The opposite vivid languages
of love and obscenity meet now in a pallid middle ground in which the
character of each is lost.* Obscene and scientific speech become practically identical, and neither of them has much to do with description
of the real world.** The success of a modern theoretical point of view
removes imagination from the realm of eros. It is another chapter in
the history of modern timidity: love is made undangerous, and those
who do the deed think that they are intellectually honest or authentic.
   The problem is not that we have too much obscenity. What we lack
is an imaginative obscenity. There are no words available for the richness of possible erotic experience—I do not say for our actual erotic

---

* So much of our language in all domains has undergone this change that there is no real original
popular speech that is not full of "role models," "values," "charisma," and many other words that
have no relation to real experience and from which we can learn nothing about it. Nor is there any refined speech that is supposed to give experiences their full due by detailed and subtle description. It
has been replaced by an abstract jargon.

** The cult of the simultaneous orgasm, which was a very important issue a few years back, is a good
example of all this. Masters and Johnson, in their clinical white smocks, treated masses of couples
who wished to achieve this feat. You can imagine what Mercutio, on the one hand, and Romeo, on the
other, would have to say about this. Their comedy and tragedy come much closer to reality. Masters
and Johnson and all of their ilk are reminiscent of Arthur Murray's Dance School with its slogan, "If
you can walk, you can dance." They think they are up to the level of Nijinsky's art.

experience, which, I suspect, is as flat as the language we use about it. It is amazing, in contrast, how many words and expressions in Shakespeare call to mind that part of our nature which is so dear to us. Not only can he teach us how to talk beautifully and amusingly about sex but he can also help us study the phenomenon much more seriously because it has not been sterilized in advance for us or put through the strainers of various ideologies. His obscenity is never reductionist. It does not dismiss the imaginative overlay of the facts. Rather, it expresses admiration for and wonder at all the strange things that happen to us in the grip of sexual passion.

Obscenity and love find expressions in Shakespeare that reveal them as two aspects of one of the most interesting of all experiences. Mercutio's "the bawdy hand of the dial is now upon the prick of noon" (II.iv.111–112) is a simile of Homeric richness that, in one of its senses, ridicules male boasting while lending itself to it. Mercutio's pricks prove him to be a shrewd and minute observer. Benvolio warns Mercutio that he will make Romeo angry with his irreverent descriptions of Rosaline's parts and what can be done to them (II.i.22). Certainly obscenity is at war with love's moral dimension, that is, the faith in fidelity, reciprocity, and the permanence of attachment. It also attacks the illusion that there can be no other object than the one that has been chosen. But it does not lead to the view that there is no natural erotic attachment. It just renders the whole experience of erotic attraction more ambiguous, and allows one to think about it. Shakespeare's speech about sex is divided between obscenity and love talk, but neither is unerotic like our casual obscenity and sexual science. In these matters, Shakespeare is fully erotic, but points to an ambiguity in eroticism. The moving innocence of Juliet and Miranda is full of a sensuality without shame. Juliet desires Romeo with her body, as Miranda desires Ferdinand. Shakespeare's obscene speakers never represent the disgustingness of the body or its desires. Rather, they glory in the wonderfulness of the senses. There is no indication in Shakespeare that eroticism is sinful, although there is plenty of indication that it reflects an incoherence and dividedness in human nature itself.

In *Romeo and Juliet* practically everybody, with the possible exception of Tybalt, is nice, and there are no villains. Good intentions are to be found everywhere, and one cannot help remembering

Saul Bellow's firm, "The Good Intentions Paving Company." Old Capulet reveals himself to be a rather decent figure, almost ready for reconciliation with the Montagues because with old age he has even forgotten the reasons for their quarrel. He forbids Tybalt to pick a fight with Romeo in his home and even repeats the local rumors about Romeo's good character (I.v.63–80). Though he plays the tyrant with his daughter, egged on by the grief surrounding Tybalt's death and by his assurance that he knows what is best for his daughter, his behavior is thickheaded but not vicious. The name Benvolio says it all. There is also an all too gentle prince who recognizes that his gentleness is a vice. Romeo, the man of love and a peacemaker, intervenes, professing his love to Tybalt, in the only really warlike scene where harm is done, and becomes responsible for Tybalt's death. The part of life where real hatred is expressed and war reigns is distorted by the well-intentioned profession of love.

And among all of these good intentions, Friar Laurence's are the best. He is usually treated as a charming and prudent man, the wise priest. He is, indeed, in all ordinary senses a nice man who maintains excellent relations with his flock. He is obviously respected by everyone, and his relationship with Romeo is especially sweet. He may be the nicest character in the play. We meet Friar Laurence musing about nature, of which he is a certain kind of occult knower. His musings in the first place argue for a harmoniousness and order in nature. All of nature is understood in its relation to man, its products being beneficial or harmful according to the way they are used. By analogy, he asserts that the conflicting principles in nature are grace and rude will. This is, appropriately to him, a Christian understanding: God is responsible for good and man is responsible for evil. But he does not, as would seem inevitable, leave it at that or, at most, attempt to tame the rude will. He, with his pharmaceutical science, actively plays God. He can mix the natural simples and serve human intentions. He is not merely a priest to whom the various persons confess but also a kind of magician. Underlying his understanding and his activity is the essence of the very gentleness that dominates the play. Everything can be harmonized (II.iii.1–26).

At the end of the friar's speech about nature Romeo enters, and their conversation proves that Romeo has taken the good friar as his confidant. The friar, as a good priest should be, is critical of Romeo's romantic enthusiasms, but he is an accomplice as well as a confessor.

One cannot take his strictures too seriously, and one might call him indulgent. A slightly more sinister element in him emerges when he agrees to marry the couple, not because he is won over to their love and for its sake, but because he sees in it the means of reconciling the two warring families. He has a political ambition, which is to do what the prince of Verona himself should have done to restore peace in the city. What he does amounts to a conspiracy in which he uses the two lovers. He cannot act directly because he is timid and without earthly power. The conspiracy, as Friar Laurence elaborates it in the contingencies of the drama, becomes ever more complex and covert. For the sake of enabling Juliet, whom he has secretly married to Romeo, to escape from the marriage her parents plan and go with Romeo to Mantua, he gives her the potion that will make her appear dead. He is a sharp contrast with the skull-and-bones apothecary, who for the sake of money defies the law by selling Romeo real poison. Friar Laurence does finally use love to make peace, but it is a peace of earthly death. As in the case of the compassionate prince, Friar Laurence seems to be a representative of what Machiavelli criticizes in Christian Italy. Earthly peace, according to Machiavelli, can be brought about only by harshness and war, not by compassion and love, and he strongly criticizes the priests for their condemnation of worldly ambition and for their spiritual weakness. They have just enough influence over the minds of men to create chaos but not enough power over their bodies to bring order.

Prior to our discussion of the denouement of the play, we should look for a moment at the two samples given to us of Friar Laurence's priestly rhetoric. When Romeo first threatens suicide on learning that he is banished, Friar Laurence suggests, without success, philosophy. That fails, so he lists the advantages and possibilities of Romeo's situation—banishment is better than death, which was required by the law but mitigated by the merciful Duke, and so on and so on. Romeo tells him that a man like him, referring to his celibacy, cannot possibly understand what Romeo faces. This whole speech is obvious and uninspired, but maybe the kind of thing any of us would say under similar circumstances. The old Nurse, who has wandered in during this scene, expresses delight at what he says, avowing that she could have "stay'd here all the night / To hear good counsel. O, what learning is." She is the priest's typical audience, this ignorant peasant woman, and she likes the sounds he makes. But he persuades Romeo only because he arranges for the first night of lovemaking. Spurred on by anticipation of great delights, Romeo for a moment forgets suicide (III.iii.54–174).

The second speech is close to comedy when Friar Laurence offers a standard set of consolations to the bereaved Capulets. They think Juliet is dead, but Friar Laurence and we know she is alive and have expectations that there will be a happy ending. He tells them that heaven has always been the destination, away from this unhappy earth. The message here is precisely opposite to the one destined for Romeo, when he tells him that life is much better than death. In addition to this decisive ambivalence, the emptiness and the manipulativeness of the friar's rhetoric are underlined by this little sermon pulled out of his file of commonplaces (IV.v.65–95).

Whether or not Friar Laurence should have married Romeo and Juliet in the first place, making use of his transfamilial and transpolitical power over the sacraments, he becomes truly blameworthy, for his elaborate machinations after Tybalt's death have made the marriage much more difficult to avow than it was before. There were two things Friar Laurence might have done if he wished to act boldly and directly. One was simply to encourage Juliet to run away to Mantua, or wherever else, with the banished Romeo. He would have accomplished the same end as he had intended to accomplish with the potion without having to rely on so many accidents governed by the great goddess Fortuna. His other possibility was to go to the families and tell them what he had done and that, like it or not, Romeo and Juliet were husband and wife. This might have been very unpleasant for him, and Juliet recognizes this when she has her terrors about drinking the potion:

> What if it be a poison which the Friar
> Subtly hath minister'd to have me dead,
> Lest in this marriage he should be dishonour'd,
> Because he married me before to Romeo?
> I fear it is. And yet methinks it should not,
> For he hath still been tried a holy man. (IV.iii.24–29)

It is really a potion and not a poison, but Juliet does point to the friar's ticklish situation. This potion is in the end equivalent to a poison for Juliet, and the priest has devised the scheme because he is too timid to be open.

One has to ask what is supposed to be gained from the whole apparent death, other than that the parents and the others concerned would be seeking a corpse rather than the living girl. The disappearance of Juliet's body would have raised all kinds of questions, as would the disappearance of her living unity of body and soul. What has happened is that a young woman has come to her confessor with a personal marital problem, and he devises, with the help of occult knowledge of nature, a miracle. This miracle is, to put it bluntly, a resurrection. Perhaps the friar believes that such a miracle would be so impressive to everyone that they would accept Juliet's infidelity to family and her choice of an enemy lover. He counts on the credulity of everyone. This is easier to do in the post-Mercutio world. Shakespeare does not permit this miracle to appear to the world at large, but it is interesting to speculate about what the opinion of that world would have been if the priest had succeeded.

The miracle fails because Romeo was not privy to the arrangement. He hears that his beloved is dead and never learns that the death is only apparent because Friar John was quarantined in Verona and never got to Mantua. Friar Laurence had not told him how essential the letter was, although it is not clear that he would have been able by dint of greater effort to have gotten it to Romeo. He clearly made no extraordinary efforts to see that the letter reached its destination. A combination of fortune and lack of foresight, perhaps due to Friar Laurence's timidity in not wanting to communicate the contents of the letter or its urgency to Friar John, results in the tragedy. Romeo rushes back, kills the well-meaning Paris, sees what he believes to be the beautiful corpse of his beloved, and kills himself on the spot. If he were less hotheaded or believed less in the appearances, the dreadful result would have been avoided, but he would not then have been the lover he was, and besides, the appearances were, of course, very persuasive.

Friar Laurence might have averted the tragedy if he had gone very quickly to the tomb. He did not, however, imagine that Romeo had heard about the death. He thinks only of being there when Juliet awakens at the end of the forty-two hours—the same time that elapsed between the Crucifixion of Jesus and his Resurrection—he has so precisely specified. He finds the awful scene, Juliet awakens, he tells her what has happened, but he hears the coming of the watch and wants to avoid capture. He tells Juliet that he will consign her to a nunnery, which seems to be the signal of the abandonment of all the earthly hope that Friar Laurence had promised. Then he commits the inexcusable crime of running away and leaving her there, when it is perfectly clear what she will do if left to her own devices. It was his simple duty to prevent Juliet from committing suicide, even though poetic necessity might dictate her death. This is the final statement about the combination of power and weakness that defines this character. His plain confession seems candid, but he apparently thinks that his good intentions exculpate him. And he takes his being scared of the arrival of the watch to be a sufficient reason for leaving Juliet. The friar is a rich study in ecclesiastical politics, and the traditional interpretation of him as a kindly old wise man will not suffice. He maintains a strange and self-contradictory view of the relation between love and death, an either / or that fails to persuade one that his "every third thought" has been the grave.

These two lovers want to live on love alone and are at least temporarily well qualified to do so. "What's in a name?" is a very good question when the names are Montague and Capulet and they live in Italy. Maybe Shakespeare intends to show us the perpetual ignorance of the conditions of happiness in lovers who cannot adjust their natures to the conventions. But there is sufficient evidence in this play that there is also something specific to this modern Italy with its imperial past, its weak but brutal independent cities, and its Church, reproduced in Shakespeare pretty much as Machiavelli described it, that affects the permanent aspects of human nature revealed in it. The sharp contrast between the gorgeous bodies and the skeletons in the tomb casts a peculiarly harsh light on hopes and realities, and the role of Friar Laurence only heightens this impression. Prospero knows this modern Italy and has suffered the consequences of its conspiratorial politics. If Ferdinand and Miranda had met in this Italy instead of on Prospero's island, they would have been just another Romeo and Juliet. Prospero can handle it all. But he is never present in a real Italy. Mercutio with his irreverence and his obscenity, his awareness that Queen Mab flatters the typical passions of lovers and priests, was a useful antidote as long as he lasted. After he departs, the alliance between love and the priest was formally fixed. At this point, we must leave this picture of the charm of love and its vulnerability and turn to consideration of a love that took place in the ancient Italian world.

chapter two

ANTONY AND CLEOPATRA

Shakespeare was the first philosopher of history. He self-consciously tried to understand the minds of men and women of the most diverse times and places, always with the view to how the permanent problems of human nature are addressed and what are the serious competing visions of the good life. The conflicts of the characters in his plays are always colored by the typical circumstances of their particular place. In commercial Venice, mercenary tolerance permits us to see outsiders in their relation to insiders better than anywhere else. In England, the struggle for legitimate kingship affects the hopes and the actions of many of his most important characters. The student who went to school in Wittenberg brings some of its theological teachings with him in his failed attempt to right the rotten state of Denmark. Shakespeare's utopia elaborated in *The Tempest,* his last play, takes place literally "no place," on an island, that is, on the stage, beyond the specific limits of real regimes. It is always helpful in interpreting Shakespeare to have a map and a chronology at hand. I suspect if anyone were to complete the task of grasping the vast plan of this most comprehensive of artists he would do so only on the basis of seeing his plays in light of time and place. Shakespeare, like a good historian and unlike historicists, needs this knowledge, not to make himself a toady of what is offered to him in the here and now, but precisely to liberate himself from it; he needs to discover the possibilities manifest in other times and places in order to live in the here and now without sacrific-

All parenthetical citations in this chapter are to Shakespeare's *Antony and Cleopatra,* ed. M. R. Ridley, Arden Edition (1954; rpt. London: Routledge, 1988).

ing his human potential. This is history as the way to discover the permanent, not to suppress it.

   The most important historical distinction for Shakespeare is between ancients and moderns. He shares the Renaissance passion for
the rebirth of antiquity and its understanding of Greek and Roman
philosophy, politics, and art. What do they say to us moderns, and can
we again get inspiration from them? These were questions of burning
intensity at the moment when the forgotten beauties of antiquity began to overwhelm the most interesting minds in Italy. It took time for
this renaissance to come to England, and Shakespeare was in a position to survey it, think it over, and apply it to his own country as well as
to his understanding of man in general. The most important difference between antiquity and modernity is, of course, Christianity. The
ancient virtues became in Christianity "splendid vices." The two
contrary moralities produced an extreme tension in the spirits of the
most interesting men and women of this time and a perhaps productive conflict in the goals of nations. We too can enter into this most interesting of worlds, if we do not assume that these were just passing
ideologies of a particular historical moment, but instead see that these
are profound and always relevant alternatives that still affect us in
various disguising syntheses. The Bible versus Aristotle's *Ethics,* or
Plato's *Republic* and Plutarch's heroes versus the prophets and the
saints, is a choice that can be as alive to us as it was to Shakespeare. It
may be true that Shakespeare presents his Greek and Roman heroes in
modern dress on the stage, but they come equipped with ancient
souls, which Shakespeare grasped in his profound readings of
Plutarch and Homer as well as others. He understood them by imitating them, and in imitating them he allows us to understand them. In
them we see the strengths and weaknesses of what is for us the most
interesting and decisively different past.

   In *Antony and Cleopatra,* a story immediately drawn from Plutarch's *Life of Antony,* Shakespeare gives us a very different kind of love
from the one we find in *Romeo and Juliet.* In the latter, we have, relatively speaking, a small-town love affair of a pair of callow youngsters.
In *Antony and Cleopatra* we have two world-historical figures, mature
and far from experiencing their first loves, acting on a stage that was for
the time the whole world. It is well for us to remember that prior to the
England that was in Shakespeare's time still just aborning, Rome was
the most extraordinary political achievement known to man—four

hundred years of republican government, and many hundreds of years afterward of imperial rule, the last reminiscences of which disappeared only a few years ago, when the kaisers and the tsars, that is, the Caesars, were pushed off their thrones. The military virtues of the Romans, unequaled by any other people, enabled them to conquer the known world, and they found the formula to make the conquests stick.

At the moment this play takes place, the republic has been destroyed, as Shakespeare depicted in *Julius Caesar*, and the great political issue is who will be the sole ruler of this empire (an empire that is simply identical to what we mean when we say the West), a struggle that is resolved in the action of the play. The issue of principle, republic versus monarchy, has been finally resolved in *Julius Caesar*. There is no dispute about the best form of government, just the question of which man has the resolve and prudence to become the sole ruler of the earth, the most complete and enticing possible prospect of political ambition, beyond that available to any other historical personages, many of whom may have dreamed it, but none of whom ever came within reach of it. It is important to note that the battle of Actium, Octavius' final victory over Antony, takes place just thirty-one years prior to the birth of Jesus and the new kind of empire connected with him that gradually took over the ground where the old kind of empire was encamped. There are two couples in the play, the enemy couple, Octavius (later Augustus) and Antony, and the loving couple, Cleopatra and Antony. Antony's presence as the common element of the two pairs indicates the high-risk and high-stakes game acted out in this play. Never before or after was love actually put in the balance to be weighed against ecumenical imperium. "Let Rome in Tiber melt" (I.i.33), says Antony at the beginning of the play. This is no idle statement. Rome could be his, and he, for a moment at least, believes that there is no contest, that love is beyond compare more choiceworthy. From the moment the curtain rises the audience must be thrilled by the grandeur of this gesture and all that it entails. The whole world, really the whole world, for a woman. Many men have idly uttered such phrases in their love talk, but no one other than Antony really could prove that he meant it. This play pushes the political and the erotic imaginations to their absolute extremes.

Shakespeare's Antony, as opposed to Plutarch's, cannot help but draw us, at least momentarily, toward a desire to have such a love. Plutarch is not indignant, but rather more contemptuous, while

Shakespeare seduces us. Antony is drinking poison, but oh how good it tastes! *Antony and Cleopatra* contains some of the lushest language in all of Shakespeare. It is less obscene than *Romeo and Juliet*, although it is suffused much more with eroticism. Mercutio's obscenity would not be alien to the classical world, but it is much more ferocious than what one finds in *Antony and Cleopatra* and is perhaps necessitated by the too sweet and secure quality of Romeo's love. Mercutio and Eno-barbus are both debunkers, but Enobarbus unabashedly tells us just how really beautiful Cleopatra is (Antony: "Would I had never seen her!" Enobarbus: "O, sir, you had then left unseen a wonderful piece of work, which not to have been blest withal, would have discredited your travel" [I.ii.150–153]), whereas Mercutio does not tell us of any such unique beauty worthy of extreme aspiration. *Antony and Cleopatra* reeks of the Oriental perfumes of the exotic extremes of Rome's empire. This is clearly a Rome that, having swallowed a world of much richer cultural diversity than it could digest, has become, in the technical sense, decadent, with no view of the future and having lost the impulse that made it soar to such heights. This is no longer the Rome we see in *Coriolanus,* where bravery and continence are everything. It is a garden that presents the most lavish display of exotic flowers in full bloom, but where the soil has become thin. There will be no restorative winter followed by a productive spring. This is a play that reminds us of the human beauty of antiquity and makes us regret the loss of it.

To reflect, once again, upon Momigliano's remark, this antiquity has the living presence of the great god Eros without the artificial imitation of it Rousseau and his Romantic followers tried to reinsert into the unerotic bourgeois world. There was within Christianity a terrible accusation leveled against this dethroned god, but even those like Machiavelli, who tried to restore the unity to man, to close the gap between the ought and the is, were pretty much willing to sacrifice the god rather than to reestablish the sacrifices made to him in antiquity. Machiavelli wrote a marvelous and obscene comedy, *The Mandragola,* which also involves a potion, the plot of which deals with a conspiracy to deceive an impotent old husband and is orchestrated by one who represents the political virtues of captains Machiavelli praises. But this very comedy indicates how unerotic Machiavelli's political vision is, for the erotic theme is meant merely to illustrate a purely political teaching concerning the impotence of Italian politics, the weakness and corruption of priests, and the opportunities existing for potential

rulers who know how to make use of fraud. Obscenity here has nothing to do with the erotic life and merely illustrates political life. When
one moves from Machiavelli to his greatest students, Bacon, Spinoza,
Descartes, Hobbes, and Locke, one sees that they have drawn the consequences of Machiavelli's teaching. Neither great reputation nor
comfortable self-preservation has much to do with eros, and these are
the motives that Machiavelli primarily recognizes in man. Shakespeare, as I contend and internal evidence strongly supports, understood Machiavelli very well and profited from that great man's
teaching, but as *The Tempest* shows, his wisest ruler used the eros for
the beautiful as a fundamental motive for his successors. *Antony and
Cleopatra* provides evidence for what caused him not to permit the
simplification of man for the sake of political purposes. He obviously
wants to promote political efficacy and the love of glory, but, as in so
many other things, he is dedicated to the preservation of the phenomenon of man. He looks all over in the best places in order to be able to
describe that phenomenon. Antony and his destructive passion for
Cleopatra are an important part of that phenomenon. Shakespeare reproduces both an austere concern for politics and a sympathy with
eros that only Plato adumbrates in the enigmatic relation between the
Republic and the *Symposium,* one apparently giving everything to politics and the other apparently giving everything to love.

The backbones of the human soul are understood by Plato to be
spiritedness, the passion of the warrior, and eros, the passion of the
lover. Antony partakes largely of both passions, two horses as they are
depicted in the *Phaedrus,*[1] but they do not seem to work too well in
harness. Love is no less ambiguous here than in a Christian context,
but it is so in different ways. Mere sensuality, if it were not allowed
to get out of hand, would be more benign than love because the issue
is not between chastity and sinning but between politics and love.
Antony's is the story of the supreme conflict between the two and,
with him, the departure of both from the scene of the world for a very
long time, perhaps up to Shakespeare's own time. This does not mean
that there were no warriors or lovers after Antony, although in Rome
itself there was left only bureaucratic regulation rather than ruling,
and sexual decadence rather than love. It does mean, however, that in
the new dispensation which overtook the world, both warrior and
lover became much more problematic, and one rarely saw them in
their pure forms any longer, let alone brought together in the soul of a

single man. Shakespeare shows us the end of antiquity in the person of Antony, and he paints a picture, warts and all, that nevertheless is intended to fill us with sympathy, admiration, and perhaps even nostalgia, if this is a sentiment in which Shakespeare indulges himself.

We see the famous couple first through the eyes of Antony's soldier friends. These men are all admirers of Antony, which is one of the main reasons we are disposed in his favor. Strong and frank men admire and love him. They know him best, and you can judge a man by his friends. Their opinion is most certainly that Antony is being destroyed by his affair. His case is treated not as though he is a sinner, but as though a great warrior is losing his martial spirit and has "become the bellows and the fan / To cool a gipsy's lust" (I.i.9–10). This is simply a soldier's judgment of another soldier, not unlike Hector's view of Paris, who leaves the battlefield to return to Helen's bed.[2] This comparison of Antony to Paris is made by Plutarch himself.[3] The difference is, of course, that Antony was, and to some extent still is, unlike Paris, a great warrior. These soldiers, as Enobarbus tells Antony, do not particularly care one way or another about his sexual escapades, but disapprove only when they get in the way of important business. To put it in Aristotelian terms, Antony suffers from immoderation, which is largely to be judged not in itself but in its effect on his capacity to act well. The category is vice, not sin, and it is a vice that can be linked with great generosity of spirit. Love—and Antony is the only man in the play who loves, and Enobarbus the only one who sympathizes with Antony in his passion—seems to be not only sensually satisfying but a sign of genial human traits in those who are its victims. Octavius, *the* opponent, is painted as utterly unerotic. Antony's response to his critics is winning:

> Let Rome in Tiber melt, and the wide arch
> Of the rang'd empire fall! Here is my space,
> Kingdoms are clay: our dungy earth alike
> Feeds beast as man; the nobleness of life
> Is to do thus: when such a mutual pair,
> And such a twain can do't, in which I bind,
> On pain of punishment, the world to weet
> We stand up peerless. (I.i.33–40)

He invokes a higher perspective in the light of which even Rome appears slight. This is not only the perspective of love; it is also not utterly unlike that of Paul, who looked at Rome in the light of the new faith. This distance on Rome's political achievements—the apparent emptiness of the goal sought with so much patience and so much blood for four hundred years, once it was attained—is something that Antony the lover and the Christians share, and Shakespeare plays on this common ground between the two, although the reasons for the contempt are so very different. This tragedy is redolent with allusions to the secular revolution taking place at the moment when antiquity has reached its peak and modernity is aborning. Soothsayers make predictions of strange new futures, and Charmian hopes to "have a child at fifty, to whom Herod of Jewry may do homage" (I.ii.27–28). The eunuch, one of the stranger products of that East where Cleopatra lives, confesses that he can do only honorable things but has fierce thoughts, and Octavius himself asserts that the day of the olive branch is at hand and that there will be universal peace. Antony is the precursor of the new order as one of love; Octavius is the precursor of it as one of peace. At the climax, soldiers hear trumpets underground and say that they signal the departure of Antony's god, Hercules (IV.iii.15–16). New gods, in no way affectionate toward Antony, will take Hercules' place. Antony's East is where the new religion will come from after he fails, a part of the world full of miraculous possibilities.

Meanwhile, Antony and all his friends are having a wonderful time in Egypt. They drink, they feast, and they make love. It is for them heaven on earth. The picture of the regal Antony and Cleopatra roaming the streets together at night, spying on the pleasures of the common folk, is most enticing. But Antony is clearly a divided man who is uncomfortable in his neglect of his imperial responsibilities. He is not like those later emperors, monstrous men who could devote themselves to monstrous pleasures without too much risk. Antony is not a monster, and he is not yet sole ruler. There is much mopping up to do. He is always on the defensive and has little of the gaiety one finds in Cleopatra or in either of their own entourages. His friend Enobarbus gets a great kick out of Antony's revels, and reproaches him only when he lets a woman get in the way of serious work. Antony seems aware throughout that his involvement with Cleopatra is fatal, but always, as he says, "I' the east my pleasure lies" (II.iii.39). This sense of evasion of responsibility makes him weak in the face of Octavius. He freely admits his guilt and agrees to change his conduct. He is like an apologetic boy facing a reproving parent. He seems to forget the strength of his position, which Shakespeare insists on. He is the only real fighter and general of the triumvirs, he has loyal troops, and in spite of mistake after mistake, like allowing the younger Pompey to be destroyed, he would still have been able to beat Octavius. But his energy is sapped by his love, as is his self-confidence. Almost everything in Antony's defeat is attributed by Shakespeare to his love for Cleopatra.

Antony is, in both his virtues and his vices, an outsized character. His voracity for all the richest experiences of glory and love is enormous. He was ruthless on his road to power and remains capable of great cruelty. He is avid of his honor but careless of many of the details of ordinary decency. He is typical of the late republic in his political criminality and his personal licentiousness. He behaves like an Olympian god, beyond the limits of the moral virtues. There is hardly a hero more impure for whom Shakespeare gives us any sympathy. Shakespeare depicts him as an extraordinary example of the classical morality of unswerving loyalty to friends and implacable hatred of enemies. Shakespeare's dislike of moralism makes him capable of taking this antique type so seriously.

Antony and Cleopatra are enchanted with each other and unabashedly want to have sexual intercourse with each other as much as possible. The act itself and the way they do it are supposed to be memorials of their sovereign superiority. I believe there is no similar example of a love without marriage sympathetically depicted in Shakespeare's plays. It is a love utterly without modesty. Antony, it must be remembered, is a married man whose wife, Fulvia, is quite a force of nature, constantly starting up civil wars on her own. Antony wants her dead but cannot help admiring her and, at least for a moment, regretting her when she dies. Cleopatra torments him endlessly about Fulvia, and when she hears that Fulvia is dead, responds with the stunning line, "Can Fulvia die?" (I.iii.58). She fiercely demands the whole of Antony, but what the Roman Fulvia represents in Antony's life can never die. The love of Antony and Cleopatra is the perfect example of a love for its own sake, at least on Antony's part, because it can never be good for Antony as anything other than itself, and the possibility of marriage or children is never considered. It is literally lawless but undeniably admirable.

The affair is riven with all the doubts and fears that love between two persons unsupported by convention can have. Both of them have had many loves before. The fact that Antony is married to another is a great subject for Cleopatra's complaints. Cleopatra is not ashamed to advertise that she has made love to two great predecessors of Antony in the power struggles, the elder Pompey and Julius Caesar, and has even borne children to both. Her motives are ambiguous because the queen of Egypt has an interest in flattering the ruler of her Roman conquerors. Antony's deeds prove that in spite of his bad track record for fidelity, only Cleopatra involves him now. Eros has rendered him to her completely. He might, from pure self-interest or his sense of responsibility, want to break with her, but he is unable to do so, however great his motives. Still, though one can always retain some doubts about Cleopatra, the overwhelming impression is that she too is in the grip of uncontrollable passion. There is none of the simple assurance and candor of a Juliet in her. Innocence is too far behind her for her to trust in the preservation of attractions. She torments Antony endlessly and artfully in order to keep him on edge. It is not quite the game of *amour-propre,* but she makes him always worry about the significance of her moods. If he is gay she will be sad, and if he is sad she will be gay (I.iii.1–12). This is not the confident and giving love so much admired in modernity. It is utterly selfish, and perhaps reveals more accurately the true nature of love as desperate need of one for the other. The tyrannical character of the total demands made by each are proof of the terrible bonds that tie them to each other. To my mind, Cleopatra's complaint to the dying Antony, "Hast thou no care of me?" (IV.xv.60), is a more powerful statement of love than are selfless expressions of sorrow or regret. Each is directed to the other by ineluctable need. Their admiration for each other means that they must possess each other no matter what the consequences. It is a hunger and a possessiveness more powerful than any other. Few men or women are capable of such selfish self-forgetting.

Cleopatra gives ample testimony to Antony's qualities by her dispositions when he is not there and her plotting to increase her ascendancy over him. She is a consummate actress in manipulating him and constantly and guiltlessly exploits his attachments to his wife and to Rome in order to make him prove that they are nothing to him and sacrifice them in her all-consuming fire. There is no prudent balancing of considerations possible with her. She asks for everything and makes it clear that it is a stark choice between her and everything else. He must break with Fulvia in order to prove his thralldom to her, and yet when he wishes to break with Fulvia, that proves he is a man of no faith. Cleopatra's servant cautions her that she is overdoing it, but she responds, probably correctly, that she knows how to catch and hold on to her prey. There is such a mixture of artfulness and artlessness in Cleopatra that it is difficult to choose between the interpretation that she is madly in love with Antony and the alternative interpretation that she simply enjoys her empire over this emperor. I believe that the evidence inclines toward the first of these two, but the doubt is important for Antony and for us. In general, he seems to be sure of her and, at the moments when he thinks of his duties, wishes to liberate himself in the way an opium smoker might wish to free himself from his habit. She is an Oriental goddess who ensnares her votaries. She is active only in converting those votaries, especially those who are rulers of Rome, to her cult. They are attracted by her beauty and the pleasures it promises. The relationship is akin to that between human and god, but this cult is a cult of beauty. In this sense, she is like the old gods.

Her widely alternating moods have a genuineness that astounds. She is what would today be called a real or strong personality. Only a dry or utterly unerotic man, like Octavius, would fail to have at least a fugitive attraction to her, if only to crush it for the sake of more urgent considerations. Perhaps the only time she is unappealing is when she insists on participating in the Battle of Actium and then runs away, and even then . . . Earlier when she has most vexed Antony, who must leave for Rome, she comes to herself, recognizes the necessity, and says, "Courteous lord, one word: / Sir, you and I must part, but that's not it: / Sir, you and I have lov'd, but there's not it; / That you know well, something it is I would,— / O, my oblivion is a very Antony, / And I am all forgotten" (I.iii.86–91). For men and women in love, every parting is a little tragedy reminding them of death, of the final inconceivable separation of those whose bodies and souls are entwined in such a way as to produce the illusion that they are inseparable. When she is alone, she glories in his memory and can think only of his virtues, virtues exceeding those of Pompey and Caesar, whom she loved in her "salad days, / When I was green in judgment, cold in blood" (I.v.73–74). Her beating of the messenger, who brings the news of Antony's marriage to Octavia, a classic example of the misplaced blame that stems from anger, suits her regal superiority to reason and further illustrates her resemblance to the old gods. In spite of the messenger's reminder that "I that do bring the news made not the match," and Charmian's saying that the man is innocent, Cleopatra asserts that "Some innocents 'scape not the thunderbolt" (II.v.67, 77). According to Hobbes, the old gods were admired not for their justice but for their power, and Cleopatra's behavior confirms this observation.[4]

She frequently uses an unadorned erotic language that seems to need no veil of mystery to be enticing. "O happy horse to bear the weight of Antony!" (I.v.21). "Ram thou thy fruitful tidings in mine ears, / That long time have been barren" (II.v.24–25). And, in a complaint that hints at what it is that makes Antony different from Cleopatra and makes her impotent to overcome the difference, "I would I had thy inches, thou shouldst know / There were a heart in Egypt" (I.iii.40–41). Heart and organ would necessarily for her express the same thing. Her sexual allusions are not like those of the serving people in *Romeo and Juliet,* filthy thoughts that have no relation to reality, nor are they like Mercutio's demystifying jabs. They are the full expression of her mode of being at its highest. She is eroticism itself. What an interest in and taste for women Shakespeare had, giving us Juliet and Miranda at one end of the spectrum and Cleopatra at the other, with an astonishing variety in between! The Romantic imagination looks very thin when compared with this.

Unlike *Romeo and Juliet,* where the beauty of the principals is attested to only by them, *Antony and Cleopatra* has the blunt truthteller Enobarbus, who is the very model of *bon sens,* tell Agrippa and us, in some of the most gorgeous poetry written in any language, of how Cleopatra "purs'd up his heart upon the river of Cydnus" (II.ii.186–187). This is an eyewitness account intended to buttress or give authority to the rumor of Cleopatra's being "a most triumphant lady" (II.ii.184). Enobarbus immortalizes the first meeting of Antony and Cleopatra when she arrives on the famous barge. Shakespeare proleptically follows Lessing's rules about the limitation of poetry in representing bodily beauty. Lessing teaches that painting cannot adequately imitate Homer's description of Helen's beauty as seen through the eyes of men who are old and have suffered because of her but who are nevertheless aroused by her. Lessing asserts that a painting which imitates this famous scene in the *Iliad* could show only superannuated lechers looking at a veiled woman. The great ancient artists illustrated this scene by making a statue of the most beautiful naked woman their art was capable of. This was the visual equivalent of the poetry. The sculptor cannot reproduce the actions but must present the essence of what the poet is saying, the impression of surpassing beauty. Similarly, the poet cannot stop his narrative, which is essentially in movement, to give off a list of the various parts of Helen's body, which can in no sense rival the immediate perception of the whole form. This would require a cold act of addition on the part of the reader, which is alien to the immediacy of the experience of actually seeing a surpassingly beautiful woman. The poet must put the experience that he wishes to convey into actions, effects on others, and so on, if, in this case, he wants to rival the sculptor.[5] Enobarbus describes the arrival of the barge and the stunning effect of its movement:

> the oars were silver,
> Which to the tune of flutes kept stroke, and made
> The water which they beat to follow faster,
> As amorous of their strokes. (II.ii.194–197)

And then we impatiently await description of Cleopatra herself, but are both delighted and frustrated by:

> *   For her own person,
> It beggar'd all description: she did lie
> In her pavilion—cloth of gold, of tissue—
> O'er-picturing that Venus where we see
> The fancy outwork nature. (II.ii.197–201)

Shakespeare refuses the temptation to do what his art cannot do well and instead reminds us of a picture, here asking us to think of any picture of a beautiful woman or goddess that we may have seen.

This last quotation contains one of Shakespeare's most interesting reflections on the relation of art to nature, the kind of reflection too many modern critics do not permit him because they think he was not as sophisticated as they are in the understanding of what art is. It is accompanied by a similar reflection put in Cleopatra's mouth:

> But if there be, or ever were one such,
> It's past the size of dreaming: nature wants stuff

> To vie strange forms with fancy, yet to imagine
> An Antony were nature's piece, 'gainst fancy,
> Condemning shadows quite. (V.ii.96–100)

This is Cleopatra's testimony in favor of Antony to balance Enobarbus' testimony in favor of her. In both cases, nature begins by being considered as low stuff upon which the artistic imagination improves. The artist presents us with a perfection that we ordinary people never encounter in life, although it follows a path indicated by our desires, fed with experiences of nature. Our longing for perfection would appear to depend on artists for its satisfaction. But there is a peripety: these human beings, Antony and Cleopatra, who are not gods, outdo anything art could hope to do. We are prepared, and our desires are sharpened by the artist's superiority to nature in its crude form, to see nature as perfection, which art then imitates. The artist is with respect to nature both humble and sublime. I wonder if this view is that much less satisfying than that of nineteenth- and twentieth-century artists who are so proud of their superiority to nature and the power of their art. These reflections on nature are most suitable to a tragedy that seems to be meant to remind us of nature.

Nature is still the theme as Enobarbus continues:

> and Antony,
> Enthron'd i' the market-place, did sit alone,
> Whistling to the air; which, but for vacancy,
> Had gone to gaze on Cleopatra too,
> And made a gap in nature. (II.ii.214–218)

Nature itself goes to accompany Cleopatra, and the passage concludes with words of almost unbearable longing:

> MAECENAS: Now Antony must leave her utterly.
> ENOBARBUS: Never; he will not:
> Age cannot wither her, nor custom stale
> Her infinite variety: other women cloy
> The appetites they feed, but she makes hungry,
> Where most she satisfies. For vilest things
> Become themselves in her, that the holy priests
> Bless her, when she is riggish. (II.ii.233–240)

I do not say that Shakespeare means Cleopatra to represent nature itself, but there is something here of the ancient appreciation of nature
as the almost ineffable standard by which all that time and custom can
do is measured. There is nothing in this view of nature to remind us of
the abstract, teleological nature that pedants speak of, a nature en-
veloped in a cobweb of moralistic abstractions that strangle it. It is the
wondrous foundation that provides us with those fundamental experiences that are truly ends in themselves and which are almost always
forgotten in the lives of toiling mortals. Even the priests themselves
must abandon their moralisms to conform to her infinite variety. It is
this awareness of nature that I believe accounts for the extraordinary
beauty of this play, which stands out among so many other beautiful
plays. This tragedy bemoans the perhaps irreparable loss of such a nature, nature expressing itself not as the mountains, the seas, and the
forests, but as the microcosm, man. Antony is—as Shakespeare, over
against Plutarch, underlines—the man *par excellence* who is open to
such an experience. It destroys him, and his capacity to appreciate it is
accompanied by important moral vices in him. But Octavius, whose
world it is about to become, is utterly blind to this vista. This makes
him a perfect administrator. If one wants a model, better expressed
than Weber ever could, of what is wrong with bureaucracy, this is it.
The erotic passions in Antony are the source of his capacity to appre-
hend a human satisfaction manifestly greater than that of being the
world's sole ruler.

And here we must return to the harsh but exhilarating facts of
politics, which this play so starkly contrasts with those of love.
In order to emphasize the radicalness of Antony's choice, Shakespeare
heightens Antony's responsibility for everything that goes wrong. On
the evidence of the play, Antony was a sure winner if he applied himself to the political situation. His position is so strong that even after
mistake after mistake, he was in a position to recoup himself. But his
judgment and his resolve are so compromised by his love affair that we
see only the ashes of a man who once had superb military and political
gifts.

When we see him together with Octavius upon his return to Rome,
he has that peculiar flaccidness we have already mentioned, apparently stemming from the sense that he has behaved dishonorably. The

soothsayer speaks of Octavius' preeminence over Antony. He always beats him, even at games of chance (II.iii.10–30). Antony does not wish to confront Octavius directly, although one might judge that the sooner-or-later should be faced sooner. It is perfectly clear that we find ourselves here in a situation beyond law or simple morality. These two powerful Romans stand in a gap between regimes; the old republican laws and structures have been laid waste and the world is waiting for one of these two men to establish the empire and its new kind of legitimacy. In the absence of law, only prudence governs the situation. This is one of those extreme moments that, according to Machiavelli, teach us the true nature of politics, which does not reveal itself in the times when traditional legitimacy covers over such extremes. Treaties are made and broken here according to their momentary utility. Neither Octavius nor Antony ever gainsays that the triumvirate cannot last and that one of them will inevitably win. Three is the number of peace, two is the number of strife. It will end with the two and then the one. If the three partners were of equal power, then the overwhelming ambition of one could be checked by the self-defense of the other two. But Lepidus is the third, and he is not a real third. Lepidus is only a name without power, treated with contempt by his partners, and easily crushed when Octavius makes his move. The difference between Octavius and Antony is that the former is perfectly unified and dedicated in his pursuit of the goal, while the latter dreams that politics will take care of itself while he devotes himself to his pleasures. His dealings with Octavius are interruptions, whereas Octavius' dealings with him are the continuation of a single-minded and long-range plan. The special character of the situation is that the qualities of manliness, which were so important to Rome in its rise, are no longer necessary. Everyone, including Octavius, gives testimony to Antony's preeminence as a soldier. Julius Caesar's strengths are divided between the two rivals—Antony has the soldier's prowess and Octavius has the prudence.

If Antony found that this moment was not the time to make war on Octavius, at least he should never have strengthened the stronger. This is Machiavelli's cardinal rule, and the one most likely to be broken by the weak-willed. Above all, the younger Pompey, who was a real threat to Octavius, should not have been destroyed. Octavius needed Antony in his struggle against Pompey, whereas Pompey was not yet a threat to Antony's eastern hegemony. Politics is normally a continuous struggle with one danger succeeding another, requiring perpetual vigilance. The Roman Empire was approaching an end of politics as all enemies were destroyed. Strangely, Antony wants politics to be over right away so that he can enjoy the fruits of centuries of struggle, whereas Octavius waits in order to establish his secure hold on the empire without any such gratification as Antony enjoys, unless one can count being treated as a god as such a gratification. Both live with the prospect of a wholly new situation in which politics disappears. Antony is simply not up to living with the threat posed by Pompey, even though it is probably a political necessity.

Antony agrees readily to the destruction of Pompey, wanting only to discharge a debt of honor and then to proceed dishonorably. He then agrees to marry Octavius' sister in order to insure the uninsurable permanence of their relationship. Octavius uses his sister with perfect cynicism and shows off the unerotic political usages of marriage, while Antony hastily agrees to the union in order to put off till tomorrow what he should be facing today. Enobarbus, as in all things, sees clearly from the outset that rather than binding the two together, this marriage will separate Octavius and Antony more radically than ever. Antony will abandon Octavia, and Octavius will be able to use this pretext for his war on Antony.

In one of the truly perfect scenes in which this play abounds, we see Pompey rejecting the empire of the world on moral grounds when it is offered to him by Menas. The triumvirs have foolishly put themselves at the mercy of Pompey by accepting the invitation to be entertained on one of his ships. This is really an illustration of what Machiavelli means by fortune, that is, putting oneself in the hands of another when one ought to keep one's own hands on that other. But perhaps it wasn't all that foolish because they could count on Pompey's morality. He is the only conventionally pious man in this play, obedient to and fearful of the gods. He is also the only one who justifies his own action in terms of republican legitimacy, calling to mind Cassius and Brutus, who fought against one-man rule. None of this has much relevance in the situation Pompey actually faces, and he himself is confused as to whether he is merely vindicating his father, or restoring the republic, or going for one-man rule himself. When Menas tempts him, proposing that they weigh anchor and slaughter the triumvirs, Pompey responds,

> Ah, this thou shouldst have done,
> And not have spoke on't! In me 'tis villainy,
> In thee, 't had been good service. Thou must know,
> 'Tis not my profit that does lead mine honour;
> Mine honour, it. Repent that e'er thy tongue
> Hath so betray'd thine act. Being done unknown,
> I should have found it afterwards well done,
> But must condemn it now. Desist, and drink. (II.vii.72–79)

This calls to mind a similar passage where Henry IV needs and wishes Richard II dead but cannot bear the responsibility of ordering it himself.[6] This is the extreme situation in which the conflict between politics and morality becomes acute, and the whole quest for justice, which should be the goal for both political and moral men, becomes questionable. This conflict can disenchant idealists and open up the field where Antonys play, indifferent to the quest for justice. I think it is clear that Shakespeare believes that Pompey makes a mistake. Though he wishes to profit from unbidden dishonorable deeds of others, Pompey holds that honor has an absolute status, a position justified only if there are gods who reward and punish. There may be a certain nobility in his stance, but if nobility has to be separated from intelligence, and depend on the spontaneous service of the ignoble, it is a pretty lame thing. Antony's heroic nobility is treated much more sympathetically by Shakespeare than is Pompey's moralistic nobility. History hardly remembers the strangled Pompey, and there is not the slightest indication that the gods took on his case. His fame in the world would have been splendid if he had performed the daring deed, and he could have worried about his reputation for justice when he was the sole ruler. He was in the jungle or the state of nature, kill or be killed. He was a pretty good lion but a complete failure as a fox. Fraud was beneath him, and he became its victim. Certainly the nobility and choiceworthiness of the political vocation become doubtful in this perspective. Shakespeare learned very much from Machiavelli's teachings about politics, but unlike Machiavelli, when the splendor of politics is suppressed he could not take politics fully seriously. This may have been the point at which he parted company with Machiavelli and became sympathetic with Antony's eroticism, which links Antony to the poet. When being a Roman was no longer an honorable qualification, the nobility of being the ruling god of the world vanished.

Just after this capital scene, which illuminates the nature of politics, there is another one that is a footnote to this one (III.i). Ventidius, Antony's subordinate, has subdued the Parthians, that previously unsubdued people on the borders of the empire who were a real and immediate threat to Antony's part of it. When Silius suggests to Ventidius that he pursue his advantage over the Parthians, Ventidius responds that it is not a good idea for a subordinate to outshine his master. The master would likely be jealous of the light that puts the master in the shadows. It is dangerous for the subordinate, who then is willing to sacrifice his master's true good for the sake of his own preservation. Envy and jealousy are ugly passions that appear in politics and undermine common goods and loyalty. Moreover, this scene raises the question about the glory attaching to great captains, for it is frequently borrowed from the deeds of subordinates. This may very well tempt the subordinates to overthrow the captains or to serve them ill. Such things were controlled and channeled when there was a functioning republic. But in the naked individualism of anarchy, they make us doubt the possibility of genuine attachments in politics.

The peak political moment in *Antony and Cleopatra* is, of course, the Battle of Actium (III.vii.7–10), where Octavius definitively becomes Caesar, his adoptive father's name, which supersedes "king" as the title of monarchs. His victory is utterly Antony's fault. Cleopatra wants to go to war; Enobarbus opposes it as vigorously as he can; and Antony takes it for granted that his female partner should go to war with him. Enobarbus, and everyone else, wants to fight on land, where Antony's superiority lies. Cleopatra wants to fight at sea, and again Antony, without question, simply follows her. The sea seems to be the element of fortune, and the land that of virtue, military virtue. It was on Pompey's ship that the three pillars of the world lent themselves for a moment to fortune. Now Antony risks himself on the sea and loses everything. He belonged to that tradition of Spartan and Roman land fighters who went to war on foot and who the ancient thinkers believed were the most reliable foundations of stable republics. In Athens, the move from land forces to sea forces during the Persian wars introduced the tumultuous democracy. In Shakespeare's time, following Machiavelli, there was an attempt to reintroduce an art of warfare that could rival the ancients. The lack of the ground soldiers who faced the enemy hand to hand was symbolic of the weakness of soul in modern man since the decline of Rome, with its bodily and spiritual arms. Antony had an "absolute" superiority on land, but this captain put a female captain over him. Yet he could have won, had not Cleopatra panicked and run away with her ships. And here is the core of it all. Plutarch quotes someone who said that the soul of a lover lives in the body of another, and in the same context he compares Antony's conduct to that of the recalcitrant black horse in the soul described by Socrates in the *Phaedrus*.[7] No doubt Antony is in love. From the point of view of sound reason, Antony is wholly to blame. When Cleopatra asks Enobarbus whether she or Antony is at fault for the defeat and the death of both now in prospect, Enobarbus answers, "Antony only, that would make his will / Lord of his reason" (III.xiii.3–4).

Enobarbus is a marvelous fiction of Shakespeare. He is made out of whole cloth, the only character who bulks much larger in Shakespeare's play than he does in Plutarch's *Life of Antony*, where he is mentioned in passing, without any characterization. Shakespeare makes him epitomize the friends of Antony, to whom one could speak so directly, thus proving Antony's capacity for friendship, for leaping over the barriers of inequality that make friendship so rare a thing for political rulers. Octavius appears to have advisors, perhaps flatterers, but no friends. Julius Caesar tried, but obviously failed, to keep his old republican equals, like Brutus, on a footing of equality when he topped them all. But Antony, as he could love, also could be a friend, and perhaps this is another aspect of his unworthiness to be king. Enobarbus represents that classical view of reason as the governor of the passions rather than their handmaiden. The contemporary parody of reason as mere calculation is a consequence of this later view of reason. The ancient view meant that the passions, none of them evil in themselves, are to be ruled and used for the sake of the good and the noble. This implied a reflection on the good and the noble that is something other than mere calculation.

At the risk of superficial schematization, I would say that the classical view was succeeded by a Christian one which believed that the passions are both irresistibly powerful and hopelessly corrupt and that reason is too weak and too deceptive an instrument to master them. They can be held in check only by fear, sense of sin, conscience, and guilt. The early moderns accepted the primacy of the passions but

tried to cleanse them of guilt and gave reason, in a new function as
scout or spy of the passions, an honorable place in the scheme of
things. But reason, the prudent ruler of the divinatory but disorderly
passions as the object of meditation, was never restored. The crisis of
ruling in the soul and its incapacity to function without consent of the
passions is paralleled by a similar crisis in politics. Shakespeare, here
represented by Enobarbus, never, even when he is making love appear
most enticing, ever takes the side of passion against reason, as would
a Romantic. The reasonable people in Stendhal's *The Red and the
Black,* Flaubert's *Madame Bovary,* and Tolstoy's *Anna Karenina* (unlike Austen's *Pride and Prejudice*) are only contemptible bourgeois.[8]
With Shakespeare, the old dignity of reason as a perfection of man is
present, and the momentary passions of a Julien Sorel and Mme. de
Rênal would never be considered by him to be a self-sufficient fulfillment. We would need much reflection on the ancient view of reason in
order to make its claims plausible, but those claims peep out in Shakespeare's plays, which deal with the extreme passions of acting men
and women. Enobarbus admires Antony. He treats his debauches as
the proper amusements of a warrior and can share at the deepest level,
as we have just seen, his erotic attractions. But he is contemptuous of
the unreason of Antony, and becomes its severest critic when Antony's
love destroys his empire and his friends:

> I see men's judgments are
> A parcel of their fortunes, and things outward
> Do draw the inward quality after them,
>
> .   .   .   .
>
> Caesar, thou hast subdued
> His judgment too.
>
> .   .   .   .
>
> A diminution in our captain's brain
> Restores his heart; when valour preys on reason,
> It eats the sword it fights with: I will seek
> Some way to leave him. (III.xiii.31–33, 36–37, 198–201)

The conflict between loyalty and reason becomes the source of Enobarbus' personal tragedy, but he is the voice of reason in this play. The
difficulty is connected with Shakespeare's obvious sympathy with
Antony's erotic passion.

In order to think well about this we should have to understand Plato's *Phaedrus*, where Socrates takes a firm stand on behalf of eros and its immoderation against the moderate, and at least apparently rational, calculations of a nonlover or a lover who wishes to appear to be a nonlover in quest of sexual gratification without madness. The praise of madness can be understood only to the extent that reason itself must be informed by an apprehension of the beautiful or the good in order to be truly what it is. In his most explicit passages about philosophy, Socrates treats it as an erotic activity, nay, *the* erotic activity. Such an understanding of reason and philosophy is entirely absent from all modern thought. That famous black horse is a recalcitrant but essential part of the upward motion of the soul's chariot. Something like this seems to be at the root of the reasonable Shakespeare's sympathy with Antony's erotic mania and his nostalgic backward look at an experience that had disappeared from the world. Antony is ruler, as were many great Romans, and lover, as were few or none. He could not harness the two, and both went down together with him.

Enobarbus chronicles Antony's fall in the name of reason, but he does something else very important in addition. In a play where the actors reflect on their historic roles and their places in posterity, Enobarbus acts as Antony's witness. In this he is entirely unlike those witnesses who were just about to appear on the eastern edge of Antony's empire. He gives testimony to the hero Antony was, a testimony that makes Antony survive the disaster of his cause. After the defeat at Actium, Antony's deterioration poses an insoluble problem for Enobarbus. Enobarbus' asides are continuous hints to us about Shakespeare's intentions:

> Mine honesty, and I, begin to square.
> The loyalty well held to fools does make
> Our faith mere folly: yet he that can endure
> To follow with allegiance a fall'n lord,
> Does conquer him that did his master conquer,
> And earns a place i' the story. (III.xiii.41–46)

Telling a story, a sort of alternative Gospel, about the old lost world is of imperative importance for Enobarbus. The suicide of a Cato in

the name of the republic, an intransigent refusal to accept the wave of
the future, was easy compared with what Enobarbus faced. For Cato,
the principle was unquestionable, whereas Enobarbus had to memo-
rialize the example of a kind of man, not as such connected to a principle, decaying before his eyes. He proves unequal to the task, but in
doing so, succeeds at it. He defects to Caesar. And Caesar is not just the
man Caesar. He is a whole new world containing new kinds of aspiration or perfection. Enobarbus quickly recognizes that this is not a
world in which he can comfortably live, that there is no place for him
in it. With one of those extraordinary gestures of antique generosity,
Antony sends after him to Caesar's camp all of the treasure Enobarbus
has left behind, together with some of his own and gentle adieus. Enobarbus is finished. The old world is no longer viable; the new one is
unbearable. And he goes to find some ditch to die in. "I am alone the
villain of the earth . . . " (IV.vi.30–39). Enobarbus makes Antony the
cynosure of posterity's eyes.

The transformation of Octavius into Caesar Augustus, who
ruled for so long and became a god more securely than did Julius
Caesar, the first Roman man to become a god, is chronicled in *Antony
and Cleopatra*. The status of god is attained when companions and followers turn into worshipers, when authority is unchallenged. This is
godship seen from the point of view of the votaries. From the point of
view of the one who becomes a god it is unrivaled and unquestioned
authority and the power to live as one pleases. No man can challenge
such a god. He represents a conclusion of the dialectic of master and
slave with the establishment of a universal master. All fear him, and all
esteem him. There is no longer a Coriolanus looking for an Aufidius to
challenge him. There are no Aufidiuses left. Octavius is an unprepos-
sessing candidate for the godhead. Without having had to perform
Julius Caesar's deeds, he picks up his legacy. In *Julius Caesar*, one sees
how Caesar found his worshipers. They were the Roman plebs for
whom he provided bread and circuses and who had no greatness of
soul with which to challenge him. He was their benefactor, and the
great-souled aristocrats were annihilated. There remained millions of
slaves and one master, whose protection was sought by all. Octavius
simply had, in an efficient and single-minded way, to confirm the result that Caesar's genius had prepared. Manliness, the very meaning

of the Latin word "virtue," was, at the beginning of this play, on the point of vanishing. The Roman Empire became peopled by a race of, as Gibbon said, pygmies.[9] In this vast space, another new God was soon to establish His authority, taking the place of the many old gods, the departure of one of which we see in this play, the manliest of them all (IV.iii.15–16). The new religion was to be eagerly embraced by the new breed of Romans. Cleopatra, while preparing her escape from Caesar's realm, for a moment acts the part of one of his worshipers. She calls him the sole ruler of the world, confesses her sexual sins, and recognizes his right to all of her property. His will is the only law. He describes the vista he overlooks when he says, "The time of universal peace is near: / Prove this a prosperous day, the three-nook'd world / Shall bear the olive freely" (IV.vi.5–7).

Octavius is the spirit of history. Throughout the play, Octavius is characterized as lacking any charm whatsoever. He is calculating, self-righteous, hypocritical, merely manipulative in his expressed indignation at the treatment of his beloved sister, unbelievable in the tribute he pays to his fallen opponents, whom he praises only for the sake of building himself up, unerotic, and a party pooper. He is by no means an evil man in Shakespeare's gallery of villains. He is merely the victor who proves the kind of mediocrity men are willing to worship when it succeeds. There is no possible earthly escape from his new modes and orders. However, in Enobarbus, Antony, Cleopatra, and Shakespeare, he ran into nonhistoricists who did not throw in their lots with the providential march of history. He is very eager to prove to the world that he acted justly. From the outset, his concern, in addition to defeating Antony, is to put him in the wrong and show that in spite of Caesar's forbearance, Antony, and anyone else who opposes him, is in the wrong. He takes people to his tent to show them what he has written to and about the other principals and his struggles with them (V.i.71–77). So much depends upon telling his story and giving the color of justice to his victorious enterprise. Enobarbus, Antony, and Cleopatra each want to tell the story of their side without any hope of its victory, intransigently insisting on the superiority of the failed cause. The rest of the play is devoted to the heroes' response to Octavius' ascendancy. Act IV is devoted to Antony's exile and suicide, Act V to Cleopatra's agony and suicide. Suicide is a great theme in *Julius Caesar* and *Antony and Cleopatra*. One must remember that suicide is a sin in Christianity, and that in Shakespeare's time this was still taken very seriously. The Christian interdiction of suicide could be understood as an attempt to make it impossible to escape God's justice. But there is not a trace of disapproval of these deeds in Shakespeare's presentation of them, and, upon reflection, one can only come to the conclusion that Antony and Cleopatra did the right thing. Suicide was very much a Roman deed, not in the modern style of "the right to death" for people whose bodies no longer work. Nor is it quite like the antibourgeois display of willingness to die, a kind of negative demonstration that one has the wherewithal to be dedicated to a cause even if one doesn't have a cause. These Romans die for country, for liberty, and for honor, not for showing that they could die. Shakespeare's characters all lived in a world, as Churchill described it, where "All had to be endured, and hence—strangely enough—all might be inflicted."[10] There are, of course, cowards in Shakespeare, but most are men who are willing and expect to fight and know that death is always a possibility in a fight. None of them quite likes to die, but they have a certain resignation in the face of the risk of death. Only in the bourgeois world does the risk of death take on an almost erotic attractiveness and become a kind of game to prove that one is not a bourgeois, the typical inhabitant of a world where the right to life is the premise of human action. There is no such right in Shakespeare. Suicide is the proof not of willingness to die but rather of a man's love of freedom, the unwillingness to bend the knee to a tyrant. The suicides in this play are committed not in the name of republican liberty, but in the name of personal freedom from the Caesarean machine. Cleopatra says, "and then, what's brave, what's noble, / Let's do it after the high Roman fashion, / And make death proud to take us" (IV.xv.86–88).

No doubt, this kind of suicide is problematic, especially as it shows concern for the opinions of others. Even in their suicides Antony and Cleopatra are engaged in a struggle with Octavius, who wants to use them as part of his victory. At the very least, they elude him by not permitting him to dispose of their fates as he wishes. Cleopatra will not be marched through Rome in a triumph, the symbol for the mob of the ridiculousness of opposing Caesar. This indicates that the intention of these suicides is not only to frustrate Caesar, but to affect the opinion of the mob.* The contempt for the opinions of the many is part of

---

* What historicists call History is for Shakespeare only a meaningless succession of mob opinions. When one understands such opinions in this way, concern for them is less justified. No one would want to miss out on the revelation and progress of the Truth. Such a view of things unbends the will to resist in the name of personal conviction.

Greek and Roman aristocratic taste, but classical aristocrats do worry about the opinions of their equals. They may even have to worry about their appearance among the mob, since only through mobs will one's memory be preserved for the special few in after times, as Cato became a model for those who wanted to found republics again, millennia after he committed suicide. Something like this surely preoccupies Cleopatra, if not Antony.

This concern for the honors accorded by others, honors that the proud man thinks he deserves whether others actually accord them or not, is a kind of Achilles' heel in the political man's makeup. Officially, at least, Socrates would be absolutely indifferent to what people think of him because he enjoys pleasures that in no way depend upon honor and because his pleasures are incomprehensible to all those who cannot partake of them. Antony shows some awareness of a possibility of such a life that is both fulfilling and outside of the system of honor when he asks Caesar for permission to live as a private man in Athens, that gentle middle ground between Rome and Alexandria. Caesar, of course, will not permit this. Antony's great love is itself a strange mixture of the private independence of two individuals who live for each other and the public life of the ruler. He partakes of a kind of simulacrum of the Socratic experience but without its self-sufficiency, at least on this earth. And it is not to be forgotten that Socrates himself committed a kind of suicide with the intention of gaining a good reputation for himself or for philosophy.

Still, Antony and Cleopatra are splendid suicides. The agonies of these two heroes, which take up an unusually large part of the play, the crucial action having taken place in the middle of Act III, are not at all typical of Shakespeare's plays. There is suffering, sorrow, and regret here, but the abiding impression is more that of an apotheosis. This is not the end of a Macbeth or an Othello, who see that they have done terrible wrongs and have destroyed the meanings of their lives. Both Antony and Cleopatra are glad that they did what they did, and the humiliation of their defeat is counterbalanced by the assertion of the rightness of their love.

Antony has two moments of anger at Cleopatra, although he has many moments of self-deprecation about the conduct that brought him to Caesar's feet and betrayed his very loyal followers. His angers are both occasioned by the defection of Cleopatra's ships and the consequences of those defections. It would not be correct to say that he is jealous of Cleopatra, but he opines that she has played him false with

Caesar, turning his love into a foolish infatuation, unworthy of the supreme sacrifices made for the sake of it. After Actium, he finds Cleopatra apparently compacting with Caesar's ambassador. She has a record of coming to terms with rival Romans who get to the top. Her capricious behavior, "her infinite variety," makes her difficult to decipher. The defections that end the second battle persuade Antony that she has "pack'd cards with Caesar" (IV.xiv.19). But in both instances Antony is easily assuaged. Immediately after Actium, Cleopatra's tears, so much ridiculed by Enobarbus, draw forth the response:

> Fall not a tear, I say, one of them rates
> All that is won and lost: give me a kiss,
> Even this repays me. (III.xi.69–71)

Antony's requests for kisses are not to be compared to Charles Bovary's, although both are made at moments of defeat.

The reversal of his fortunes unhinges Antony, and he becomes extremely erratic. His worst moment is when he challenges Caesar to a single fight, rebelling against the unfairness of a poor fighter's winning out over a good one. Caesar answers simply, "let the old ruffian know, / I have many other ways to die" (IV.i.4–5). He also induces his followers to cry for him, of which he is immediately ashamed. But underneath it all there is this continuous stream of erotic feeling for Cleopatra. Even his great speech comparing himself to the illusions projected by the clouds, insubstantial things that quickly dissipate, ends in their mutual expectation of embraces in heaven. At the very end, he says,

> I am dying, Egypt, dying; only
> I here importune death awhile, until
> Of many thousand kisses, the poor last
> I lay upon thy lips. (IV.xv.18–21)

Antony is easily persuaded by Cleopatra's mere speech that she did not betray him at Actium. He has really tragic suffering just after the second battle and the desolation induced by his belief in Cleopatra's dishonesty. He cries out that he is suffering, as did his ancestor hero and god, Hercules, in the shirt of Nessus. His contemplated suicide is at this moment simply the end of everything. But he is mollified when he hears that Cleopatra has preceded him. He then thinks only of joining her. The fact that this is just one of her tricks and that she is still very much alive may cast some light on the genuineness of love, but certainly Antony, even provoked to the limit, always gently returns to his dedication to this woman. And he is vindicated by her extraordinary behavior in the scenes after he dies. They are joined to each other forever. It is one of those marvelous historical accidents that Antony had a servant named Eros, and throughout Act IV his calls for the help of his servant, Eros, Eros, stud his speeches. "Eros!—I come, my queen!—Eros!" (IV.xiv.50) is typical of these passages. Antony wants Eros to kill him, but Eros commits suicide himself, thus depriving Antony of a death administered by Eros. He must do it himself, and he half botches the job, which allows him to spend a delicious last moment with his beloved. The richness of the allusions contained in this, the death of Eros, needs no commentary.

Antony's struggles and his farewell to this world concern fortune and Caesar. In a sort of Stoic reflection on fortune, he recognizes that human autonomy requires independence from the turns of its wheel. Caesar's happiness depends not upon Caesar but on fortune, and Caesar can tomorrow become a slave. This is Brutus-like, and a certain aping of wisdom. Anyone devoted to politics depends on fortune. Antony's attachment to eros surely reduces that dependency, but this is all part of the incoherence that brings him down. He reiterates the importance of suicide—"a Roman, by a Roman / Valiantly vanquish'd" (IV.xv.57–58)—as part of his independence of Caesar. This is a noble stance, but it rings somewhat hollow. However, Antony, a much less moral man than Brutus, is actually more independent of the political wheel of fortune than is Brutus, and this is undoubtedly due to his love. Brutus dies for an utterly lost cause, whereas Antony has at least for a moment participated in beauties that never change, and in the end dies because of and for them.

Actually, Caesar does not care about bringing Antony back to Rome to decorate his triumph. He simply wants him dead. "We could not stall together, / In the whole world" (V.i.39–40). But Antony does believe that his story will be different from Caesar's. Caesar's world depends on capturing everything that would oppose it. Actually, Antony's story, as something independent of Caesar's and choiceworthy for its own sake, depends on Shakespeare.

Shakespeare makes Cleopatra into Antony's historian as she struggles to come to terms with her loss:

> It were for me
> To throw my sceptre at the injurious gods,
> To tell them that this world did equal theirs,
> Till they had stol'n our jewel. (IV.xv.75–78)

They have had heaven on earth, but the jealous gods have deprived her of her earthly god. But by the end of Act V, she has "immortal longings," and goes to meet her husband in heaven. She is upset that Iras precedes her, for fear that she take the kiss from Antony that was destined for her. The mortality of love between two human lovers is not acceptable to her. She and Antony join in the divine union after death that is required by their love. They both long for immortality, as eros always prompts man to do according to Socrates, but they are able to seek for it only in mortal individuals. From their experience with each other, they divine the divine, but do not grasp it. They are right in thinking that it is eros in man that leads toward the divine and that, unlike many other visions of the divine, it must begin in the divine form of man. Cleopatra's descriptions of Antony, from the moment of his death to her own, are overpowering. His last words to her were intended to justify her love of him. She never needed to justify herself to him because she was the lovable in itself. Her praise of Antony is only heightened by the fact that it is interspersed with flattery of the new god of the earth, Caesar. One is thus forced to compare him with Antony, the god of her soul. Their movement to heaven does not quite persuade us, but we cannot help wishing them well. This is another kind of divinity produced in decadent Rome.

And, finally, again the question of who is to enjoy that famous triumph. All of Antony and Cleopatra's worshipers have converted to Caesar, who says that the converts alone would be enough with which to defeat Antony. With the exception of the regretful Enobarbus, these conversions are painted as low things, the generality of mankind's worship of vulgar success. Cleopatra's passion not to be incorporated in that success, not to be one of those defeated without dignity by the new order of things, is overwhelming:

CLEOPATRA: Now, Iras, what think'st thou?
> Thou, an Egyptian puppet shall be shown
> In Rome as well as I: mechanic slaves
> With greasy aprons, rules, and hammers shall

Uplift us to the view. In their thick breaths,
Rank of gross diet, shall we be enclouded,
And forc'd to drink their vapour.
IRAS: The gods forbid!
CLEOPATRA: Nay, 'tis most certain, Iras: saucy lictors
Will catch at us like strumpets, and scald rhymers
Ballad us out o' tune. The quick comedians
Extemporally will stage us, and present
Our Alexandrian revels: Antony
Shall be brought drunken forth, and I shall see
Some squeaking Cleopatra boy my greatness
I' the posture of a whore. (V.ii.206–220)

Caesar is indeed robbed and disappointed when Cleopatra escapes
him. He puts the best face on it when he says, "and their story is / No
less in pity than his glory which / Brought them to be lamented"
(V.ii.359–361). They are now objects of pity, brought to that condition by Caesar, whose glory, Caesar insists, is enhanced by his having
done so. But what Cleopatra most feared does not come. In this play,
she is "boyed" (the most improbable role for any of the boys who
played women in Shakespeare's plays), but not as a whore. It is only in
Caesar's tradition that a Cleopatra would be indistinguishable from a
whore. Shakespeare picks up the cause of Antony and Cleopatra, and
by his poetry perhaps leads us to the truest meaning of eros. Generation after generation they are renascent on a stage on this earth, and
thus Shakespeare pricks our heart with longing, not for a lost world,
but for something that is always accessible to man as man. This is really a triumph.

chapter three

MEASURE FOR MEASURE

Measure for Measure is another play that is dominated by a priest's plot, but, unlike the plot in *Romeo and Juliet,* this equally contrived solution to a problem works. The happy result makes us laugh. The solution to sexual problems is comic both because it is so improbable and because coping reasonably with these desires somehow makes them look ridiculous. Perhaps the plot works because the priest is not really a priest but a genuine political ruler who uses the cloak of religion to hide himself and his designs. Political wisdom seems to require some such religious coloring in order to make itself acceptable to the unwise subjects. Certainly this false friar escapes the law's narrow concentration on men's deeds by using the Church's capacity to get inside men's thoughts.

The explicit intention of Duke Vincentio's ruse is to restore the force of law, which has for either fourteen or nineteen years been allowed to fall into desuetude. The laws in question are perhaps the most decisive of laws, those concerning sexual conduct. They appear to be the most necessary and the harshest, those that go most against nature's grain. Precisely why the Duke has neglected to enforce the laws is difficult to understand. Either he was, like Prospero, too involved with his own thought to pay attention to the unpleasant business of governing, as Escalus suggests, or, as a bachelor, he himself profited from the laxness in the city. There is a hint of this latter interpretation when Friar Thomas takes the Duke's petition for haven to be

All parenthetical citations in this chapter are to Shakespeare's *Measure for Measure,* ed. J. W. Lever, Arden Edition (1954; rpt. London: Routledge, 1988).

a request to carry on an affair in his monastic abode (I.iii.1–6). This immediate supposition on Friar Thomas' part would seem to be based on prior experience. And as we shall see, the Duke is too honest a man to be simply a hypocrite in condemning practices in which he participates. The Duke knows the legislator is beyond the law, but the law requires his conviction and support. There may be need for terror in order to put law in the seat usurped by lust, but the Duke respects nature and will not lend himself to the dishonesty required simply to deny it. The mercy that tempers the harshness of the newly reapplied law stems from the reflection that "there but for the grace of God go I," that is, both you and I have the same desires and perhaps the same experiences as those who are condemned. The law that condemns erotic activity is made by erotic men. This leads to the heart of the play's ambiguity.

Vienna is the seat of the Holy Roman Empire, and the Church, in both its purity and its corruption, is highly visible there. The Duke effects a kind of Reformation in Vienna, and the astounding fact of the play is that throughout it untamed sexual desire is accepted as a fact of life. Those who do not admit it are as much reformed as those who do.

Vienna is a sexual mess. Bawdy houses are the accepted way to get sexual satisfaction. People talk of them as they do about food markets, and take it for granted that they can be no more easily suppressed than are the food markets, which are necessary. If the proprietors and clients of the bawdy houses, or, in general, all the loose individuals, are something less than admirable, they are either merely comic, which means harmless, or pleasant persons of good company. They are not like criminals who knew they were breaking the law and got caught; they are really surprised that there can be such laws and that they are to blame.

Nobody, but nobody, is married in this town. There is no family, and marriage is not understood to be necessary for procreation. Natural children are hardly thought to be bastards, and the Christian's insistence that a child not born in holy wedlock is a counterfeit has no weight in Vienna. Escalus, a remnant of the old regime, asks Pompey whether Mistress Overdone had more than one husband. He responds, "Nine, sir; Overdone by the last" (II.i.198–199). People once had fathers and mothers, but they are gone. The extreme expression of what is sexually wrong in Vienna is that there is a great deal of venereal disease, the result of promiscuity.* The Duke apparently finds this situation intolerable. His response, as we shall see, is not "get thee to a nunnery," in either sense. He wishes to reestablish the institution of marriage, which is a mode of sexual expression, although one constrained by law. He apparently is ready to do so because he is now at the point where he is himself willing to marry. It should not be forgotten that his plot culminates in his own marriage, which would have been impossible if the reform had not taken place. What appears to be an extremely severe reform turns out to be actually a gentle one, with license given even to the houses of ill fame for the sowing of wild, that is, unlawful, oats, on the condition that they be less open and be ashamed before respectable institutions. But getting a lot of people married is the central intention of this political deed. The naturalness of marriage is questioned by the action of the play while its political necessity is affirmed.

The Duke's withdrawal from Vienna is an assumption of a god-like behavior. He is an absent god for whom a human deputy acts. This deputy is watched by another branch of the god's presence in absence, the Church and its priests. The Duke, disguised as a friar, spies out what the law would never see or take into account. This actually reveals a weakness in the written law itself and in its executors. The priest acts deceptively, dishonestly, and abuses the Church's doctrines in order to attain his ends. His behavior is innocuous in *Measure for Measure* because the priest is actually the ruler. The supplement to the law provided by the Duke's prudence, his exceptions of persons, and his privately gained knowledge of the inner life of souls would be requisite for full justice. However, its political institutionalization by means of the Church would be as fraught with difficulties as is the appointment of a deputy. Shakespeare, following Machiavelli as well as the whole classic tradition, is disapproving of the rule of priests. In this case, however, the real ruler in the guise of priest is able to make Angelo, his deputy, assume that his position is invulnerable because nobody other than Isabella knows what he has done, whereas the false priest

---

* One cannot help being reminded of Montesquieu's wry hints that the Mosaic Law is so severe, even in its dietary injunctions (Montesquieu asserts that pork is noxious for those with venereal disease), because those inhabitants of the Fertile Crescent to whom it applied were racked by venereal disease, which threatened life at its very source.[1]

knows it all. Here the Duke's disguise permits him to be omniscient, as is a god, and to manipulate and to mitigate the omnipotence of the political ruler. In extreme cases, such as the basic reform the Duke is effecting, what Machiavelli calls unusual modes are necessary and just.

The Duke's withdrawal and the appointment of an efficient and severe deputy to do the nasty business is a tactic Machiavelli applauds. He gives as an example for imitation Cesare Borgia's appointment of Remirro de Orco as his deputy when he wanted to reduce the Romagna to peace and obedience. When de Orco had successfully completed the tasks given him by Cesare, the latter,

> because he knew that past rigors had generated some hatred for Remirro, to purge the spirits of that people and to gain them entirely to himself, . . . wished to show that if any cruelty had been committed, this had not come from him but from the harsh nature of his minister. And having seized this opportunity, he had him placed one morning in the piazza at Cesena in two pieces, with a piece of wood and a bloody knife beside him. The ferocity of this spectacle left the people at once satisfied and stupefied.[2]

Shakespeare, in his sweeter way, actually imitates Machiavelli's example with his play. The punishment of Angelo is rendered more moral than was Remirro's, because Angelo is actually disloyal to his master, whereas Remirro was not. One gradually becomes aware that the Duke's purpose is as much to humiliate Angelo as to punish fornicators. As a matter of fact, the person who most suffers punishment and humiliation in the play is Angelo, a strange way to go about restoring sexual morals. Rather than being cut in half, Angelo suffers an equally fearsome fate—he must marry. The populace is impressed by both the Duke's harshness and his mercifulness. The Duke, on the one hand, acts like the Moral Majority in the sanctifying of the family. On the other, he acts like the ACLU in impugning the motives of the Moral Majority. He obviously thinks that neither is quite the right thing. The Duke tells Claudio, "Be absolute for death" (III.i.5), whereas the play is absolute for life. Aside from the hapless Claudio, the only person other than Angelo to suffer greatly in the play, in which such severe punishment threatens and in which executioners are so visible, is Isabella. And Isabella is also the only other person with high moral pretensions. Much of *Measure for Measure*'s message is conveyed when Pompey the pimp is appointed deputy executioner.

This play illustrates the humanizing of the law by making sure that it is not made by beings who have never felt the human movements of soul and body. A godlike law applied to humans rather than angels results in a perversity that is worse than lechery.

The Duke surely knows what Angelo is prior to appointing him and suggests to the more humane Escalus, more humane in that he remembers in his old age the desires he had when he was young, that he wants to see what Angelo will do. He also knew prior to the action of the play that Angelo had abandoned Mariana in spite of his pledges to her. Angelo is much worse than Claudio, who merely put off marriage until the dowry came through but remained faithful, if that is the word, to Juliet, whereas at the loss of the dowry, Angelo jilted Mariana. Still, he appears honestly tormented when he becomes attracted to Isabella. A sophistry of the heart could have allowed him to forget his bad behavior to Mariana, and there seems to have been no sexual relationship with her. There money seems to have been the theme. Whether the Duke could have counted on Isabella's attracting the attention of Angelo or not, the Duke did expect some such abuse of power. It would seem likely that her brother, Claudio, the first and only real sufferer from the reawakened law, was pointed out to Angelo by the Duke. It is not necessary to assume that Angelo is a Tartuffe, self-consciously using his reputation for piety to gain access to women.

What we see in the great scene with the lecherous Lucio, urging Isabella to heights of rhetoric, is the welling up in Angelo of an erotic attraction to the notion of corrupting virtue (II.ii.26–187). This is a perversity beyond any that might be attributed to the low persons in the play who have frank sexual attractions to good-looking persons or merely have a need for sexual release. There is a refinement in Angelo that sets his senses in motion in the presence of innocence and virginity. It is eroticism heightened and refined by its being forbidden. He confesses to himself that this is infinitely more attractive than natural sexual appeals. Angelo's imperious need for Isabella is inconceivable without the attraction of its being a sin.

The two encounters between Angelo and Isabella are the highlights of this play. He moves, in his own self-understanding, from god to sinner. Before our eyes we see the genesis of guilt. He wills and he does not will. Before, he thought that will and deed were identical in him. He elevates sexual desire into the realm of the forbidden, forbidden by his own standards and his position, and then hates himself for his sexual desire. He becomes disgusted by sexual desire in others, because he attributes to them the same criminality he finds in himself. This makes him into a criminal: he forces Isabella to have sexual intercourse with him and murders Claudio to cover up the rape. At least he thinks he commits these terrible deeds and is foiled only by the Duke's manipulation of appearances. He begins as the cold instrument of the law and metamorphoses into the only malevolent person in the play. This means he delights in doing harm while struggling with his conscience. Sinning and repenting become a way of life for him. Presenting himself as the enforcer of law on fallen man, he actually reenacts the harshness of God at the first Fall.

Shakespeare has very little sympathy for this kind of moralistic sexuality. He has a particular need to humiliate men who make claims like Angelo's. Henry V, in his typically cold fashion, uses the severe Chief Justice to punish the inhabitants of the Boar's Head Inn, especially Falstaff, with whom he has spent his youth and for whom Shakespeare has a great deal of sympathy.[3] He does so for the sake of public morals, as opposed to private satisfaction, now that he is king. He does so also to satisfy the puritanical passions that are rife among the people and which Shakespeare rightly saw would threaten civil peace. These were not the simple moral demands that frighten liberals so, but real puritanical passions of the sort that are today making parts of the Islamic world ungovernable. Something like this is what the Duke is after, though he accomplishes it much more nicely than does Hal. Not only does he wish to channel the sexual affections more or less into family attachments, but he also wants to fend off the threat of extreme reactions by Puritans, whose souls have been prepared for extremism by their religion. The sense of sin grafted on to sexual desire, not a thing to be found in Mistress Overdone's house, accounts for the distortions of Angelo's soul, and Shakespeare's dislike of Puritans is subjected here to profound and fundamental analysis. Nietzsche said, "Christianity gave Eros poison to drink. He did not die, but became vice."[4] Most of the others in the play are indulgent or dirty-minded but not perverse. It is imagination, not the body, which causes Angelo to be attracted to the conquest of purity.

For nothing in the world would Isabella sacrifice her maidenhead, and Angelo would do anything in the world to have it. So she and Angelo are, in a sense, well matched in that they both set an overwhelmingly high price on virginity. Isabella is an attractive, spirited, intelligent girl with a gift for self-righteous rhetoric. She is entering a religious order but has not yet taken her vows. The rigorous "restraints" on the behavior of the sisters are not enough for Isabella, who professes a wish for stricter ones. Her setting among the sisters provides the other pole in the stark opposition that characterizes Vienna—bawdy houses versus holy houses. The center is represented only by the weak Claudio, who floats about between looseness and the sanctity of marriage. The center does not exist in any substantial way, and the Duke's project is clearly intended to make the naturalness and goodness of sex acceptable to one kind of extremist, and to submit its wildness to the yoke of the law in the other kind of extremist. The Puritans are the hardest to persuade because they lead from moral superiority, a great self-satisfaction.

Isabella is pretty easygoing about the habits in Vienna, most probably because she feels superior to them. Her response when she hears that her brother has made a child without the benefit of law with her good friend Juliet is that they should get married. This is perfectly sensible and fits the wishes of the two parties, but it hardly fits with her view of the sacredness of virginity and the base character of those men who would wish to rob her of it. She has chosen chastity, an utter giving up of erotic satisfaction, at least with human beings, although she occasionally seems a bit confused and says that virginity must be kept only to protect the genuineness of any offspring she might have. The premise of this entire play is that there is no way to avoid sexual attraction. Angelo and Isabella, in their own ways, prove to be affected by it. The Duke, when disguised as a priest, tells the Provost that there is no danger in having an unsupervised encounter with Isabella because he is a priest. But he manifestly is attracted to Isabella. The loose must be frightened into curbing their sexual expression; the tight must be made to experience the power of sexual attraction.

As a result of her encounters with Angelo, Isabella begins to see something of the weakness of the grounds on which she stands and becomes a fanatic. She has learned of her rhetorical power under the instruction of the loose Lucio, this worthless fellow, who is more severely punished than any of the other bawdy characters in the play, but less for his sexual practices than for his insults to the Duke. She begins in her first interview with Angelo by meekly and a little too easily accepting her brother's punishment. Then at the end of the first interview, when she has begun to be enchanted with the sound of her own voice (a thing to be denied her according to the rules of the order she is entering against converse with men), she promises Angelo that if he shows mercy, she'll put in a good word with God on his behalf. The speech of Isabella that immediately precedes Angelo's first signs of attraction is intended to remind him that he too is a man and must once have had such feelings as her brother's. This is an appeal to mercy, not as divine grace but as recognition of common human frailty. But in her second interview, where Angelo, now a sexual highwayman, in effect demands, "Your virginity or your brother's life," she engages in a dialogue in which Angelo makes a few real points. She is forced to admit that she sets different standards for her brother and herself and that Angelo simply applies laws, the principles of which she accepts. More important, she is forced to agree that her refusing to have sexual intercourse with Angelo is akin to Angelo's refusal to pardon a similar act by her brother. Angelo tells her that she will be pardoned by God for the intention of her act. The outrageousness of the situation, in which the enforcer of the law is now breaking it, helps to conceal the weakness of Isabella's position. Part of the Duke's intention, as I have indicated, is to make the law, without loss of majesty, more clearly a product of human beings with human frailties and thus less tyrannical. He reduces the gap, the necessary gap, between the ought and the is. Isabella, overheated, starts using erotic language to describe her attachment to her virginity, for which she is willing to die. She says she would "strip myself to death as to a bed / That longing have been sick for, ere I'd yield / My body up to shame" (II.iv.102–104). Virginity has metaphysical status for her now. "Then, Isabel live chaste, and brother, die" (II.iv.183).

This disposition might appear to be noble, but it is understandable that her brother is not totally of Isabella's persuasion. This is perhaps because, although he seems a decent enough fellow, his sexual history makes it clear that he has always had some practical doubts about the sinfulness of sex, including its sinfulness prior to marriage. He and his fiancée, Juliet, are meant to represent the typical subjects of the law's new rigor. They consummated their marriage before it took place because the dowry was held up. Why not enjoy oneself now, since life is so short and the intentions are good? But when he is arrested, he easily accepts the justness of the law and asserts that he suffers as a result of his own licentiousness. Somehow, the principle of marriage was instilled in him, and it is easy for him to acknowledge that he should have waited. This law does not deny sexual satisfaction or make his deed irreparably sinful. Partly, he accepts it passively because he hopes that his acknowledgment of the rightness of the law will save his life. But partly he and his Juliet (who sweetly tells the Duke, when, in the guise of a friar, he is haunting the prison and moralizing with its inmates, that she now honestly regrets what she has done) represent the practice of the great majority of mankind who neither particularly enjoy frequenting prostitutes nor have an overwhelming desire to enter monastic orders. The problem in Vienna is partly structural: there is a high view that rejects sex and, perhaps consequently, a low view that simply accepts it in whatever form it is available. These ordinary people are likely, without too much anger or rebelliousness, to restrain themselves and get married. Such persons are not sufficiently erotic really to run risks, nor do they have the obsessive motives of an Angelo.

Claudio is that poor fish who is the first to suffer from the fresh vigor of a law. He tells the cop, "Why me? I was just following traffic." It is not exactly what you would call a noble stance, but it touches all those who may have once in a while broken a law that was in disuse, like buying condoms in Connecticut or committing sodomy in one's own home in Georgia (although in old Vienna, there were no lawyers trying to get the laws applied in order to get them discredited). He is scared out of his wits when Angelo, his sister, and the Duke all condemn him to death, in spite of the sympathies of the other characters who think the punishment too severe. The Duke presents one of those moralistic speeches that impress solemn people, but which, in Shakespeare, are meant to be only empty speeches for the consolation of persons in bad situations. We have seen this with Friar Laurence in *Romeo and Juliet* and now we see Friar Lodowick, aka the Duke, doing something similar in *Measure for Measure*. His speech instructs Claudio about how terrible life is and how preferable to it death is (III.i.5–41). This speech, unlike some of the other speeches of the false friar, is not Christian but Stoic. There is no talk of the afterlife or of the immortal soul. Rather, the Duke's sermon concentrates on man's nothingness and his origins in dust. Lessing, with his characteristic good taste, confesses that he never much liked Stoicism because it treats men as though they were gladiators. He denies that the calm expression on the faces of Laocoön and his son as they are being strangled by the snakes has anything to do with the denial of pain. He points out the wonderful passage in Homer where, prior to the great battle between the Achaeans and the Trojans, there was absolute calm in the Trojan camp, for "great Priam would not let the Trojans cry."[5] The Greek camp was full of wailing, which Lessing interprets as proving that the Trojans were barbarians and the Achaeans Greeks, that is, peaks of civilization. In practice, this means that Greeks could accept their tears, and yet be men and fight. Barbarians had to repress nature. I believe that almost all of Shakespeare's Stoical utterances are meant to ridicule the dehumanizing Stoic morality.[6] The contrasts are so overdrawn in the Duke's sermon that it is impossible to understand how anybody ever got any pleasure in life whatsoever. If you are young, you are too poor to have any enjoyment, and if you have money, you are too old to have any enjoyment, and so forth. The Duke denies what Aristotle readily admits, that mere life is pleasant and that is why men hold on to it. The peak of this kind of moralism is to tell you that you do not enjoy what you enjoy. It is literally unbelievable, although for a moment a man punch-drunk from the blows of fortune may say he believes it, as does Claudio: "I humbly thank you. / To sue to live, I find I seek to die, / And seeking death, find life" (III.i.41–43).

This engaging boy is scared witless. This scene prepares for Isabella's arrival in the prison and discussion with her brother about their situations, a discussion spied on by the Duke (III.i.48–149). This is Isabella's worst moment. She tells her brother how horribly she is put upon and expects him to accept, at the cost of his life, the price she puts on her virginity. *He* could not live with *her* shame on his conscience. The death of a brother is as nothing compared with the sacrifice she would have to make. She picks up the Duke's theme in telling him what a little, little thing death is. Death rather than dishonor is her theme song, but humanly, all too humanly, Claudio, and the majority of mankind, wonder whether this is so simply the case. When she makes explicit the terrible, impossible thing she is asked to do in order to save her brother's life, Claudio's resolve to die imperturbably begins to be shaken. This is a chilling scene, but, in its way, one of Shakespeare's most comic inventions. When Claudio realizes that she has no intention whatsoever of saving him by the means Angelo provides, he says with a kind of resignation, "Thou shall not do't." Isabella responds gaily that if it were only her life at stake, as it is only Claudio's life, she would throw it away as easily as she would a pin. To which Claudio responds, one can imagine in what tone, "Thanks, dear Isabella." Then Claudio begins himself to engage in the kind of scholastic casuistry that took place between Angelo and Isabella. He says that Angelo must not regard it as such a big sin, because he is a devout man who would not want to risk being punished in perpetuity for "the momentary trick." "It is no sin; / Or of the deadly seven it is the least." Isabella, in astonishment, asks, "Which is the least?" (III.i.109–111). And then Claudio, in a fully human and moving speech, tells Isabella what he really feels about his execution:

> Ay, but to die, and go we know not where;
> To lie in cold obstruction, and to rot;
> This sensible warm motion to become
> A kneaded clod; and the delighted spirit
> To bathe in fiery floods, or to reside
> In thrilling region of thick-ribbed ice;
> To be imprison'd in the viewless winds
> And blown with restless violence round about
> The pendent world: or to be worse than worst
> Of those that lawless and incertain thought
> Imagine howling,—'tis too horrible.
> The weariest and most loathed worldly life
> That age, ache, penury and imprisonment
> Can lay on nature, is a paradise
> To what we fear of death. (III.i.117–131)

Here the issue is not simply the end, no longer existing, as it is in the Duke's speech, but what imagination tells us about the things that happen after death. On the one hand, there is the rotting of one's lovely warm body and, on the other, the experiences of the soul that are told to us by poets, beginning with Homer's guided tour of Hades. Claudio speaks, as does Achilles, of being willing to accept any condition in the world in preference to being king over all of Hades. And he begs, "Sweet sister, let me live" (III.i.132). Nature, gentle nature, gives a dispensation for sacrificing one's maidenhead, as well as one's life, for a friend or a relative.

None of this is the reaction of the philosopher. Lucretius' whole philosophic effort is to persuade the persuadable, a small number, not

to be terrified of an afterlife. This liberates men from the fear of afterlife, which can ruin the pleasures of this life, but it takes nothing away
from the natural fear of nothingness. Philosophers and ordinary men
both fear death, but they do so for different reasons. The philosophers
are more inclined to accept it because they have thought it and its necessity through. This only underlines the perfectly decent ordinari-
ness of Claudio. But neither wise man nor ordinary man would very
easily accept death when salvation is so easily in their grasp. Only
those who accept the framework in which virginity is more highly
cherished than anything else could do so. Isabella's rejoinder to Claudio's touching appeal is "O, you beast!" (III.i.135). Her indignation
becomes prurient as she equates preserving life at the expense of a
sister's shame with incest. She imagines the act and invests it with
everything her religious vocation connects with it. Claudio obviously
doesn't think of it in this way but quite rationally sees his sister's
single contact with Angelo as a means to a very important end. Isabella
goes on to impugn her mother's virtue because such a man as Claudio
could never have been the son of her father. She works herself up to a
pitch where she herself condemns her brother to death all over again.

The Duke, seeing all of this, is evidently attracted to this girl,
more by her potentiality than by her actuality. He is going to
subject her to a number of trials and tortures that will have the effect of
taming her spiritedness and bringing her back into the circle of mortality. He immediately makes her privy to the part of his conspiracy
directed against Angelo. He has been cultivating Mariana for a long
time, and he proposes that she take Isabella's place at the tryst with
Angelo. The Duke, who talks only of force, always acts by fraud, and
he lies to and deceives almost everyone over and over again. He asks Isabella to participate in arranging an act of carnal knowledge. She does
so willingly, partly because she seems concerned primarily with *her*
chastity and *her* honor. The friar provides a cover of propriety by saying that a prenuptial agreement is the same as a marriage. It is questionable whether this is so, inasmuch as Claudio is being punished
with death for having had sexual relations—or is it perhaps a baby?—
after a similar agreement prior to marriage.

What can Isabella think will be the result of Mariana's having sexual intercourse with Angelo? When Isabella first hears of Mariana's

plight, with her typical generosity with the lives of others, she says that Mariana would be better off dead. It is very hard to figure out how this covert act would turn into marriage. Isabella does not demand many details inasmuch as she sees a way of saving her brother and not dishonoring herself. The Duke leaves it to Isabella to tell Mariana about the plan, a scene we do not see on stage but on which we are invited to reflect. One must wonder what the faithful Mariana felt about all of this. She is the only person in the play who manifests an undying attachment to anyone, to the man who is the least deserving of love in the entire play. Does she accept this encounter with resignation or delight at the possibility of finally enjoying the fruits of her love? There is no evidence that Angelo had ever experienced a sexual attraction to Mariana, or to anyone, before he met Isabella. Now Mariana has to accept a sexual act with her beloved that is possible only because he imagines he is doing it with someone else. This is at the very least humiliating and argues for an ambiguity in her future sexual relations with the man she hopes will be her husband. Will he ever be aroused by her, or will he always have to imagine Isabella in order to perform the act? His sexual pleasure is, at the least, greatly enhanced by the thought that it is Isabella he is enjoying. Isabella herself must be aware that Angelo will think he has had her and, in a way, will think so for the rest of his life, even though he is to learn that it is untrue. There is a whole dissertation here on the relation between imagination and reality in the commerce between the sexes. The Duke is a refined torturer in such matters. Angelo has had the experience of Isabella and will probably spend the rest of his life comparing Mariana with Isabella. And before his eyes he will see the woman he truly lusted after enjoyed by the Duke. Perhaps the lesson is that these things are all the same in the dark, but Angelo will never believe that. This would be the philosophy of Mistress Overdone's house. The Duke is diabolical.

Isabella, after having acted so efficiently in arranging an act of sexual intercourse, is almost immediately rewarded with the announcement that her brother is dead. Perhaps it is necessary for the Duke to use Isabella's indignation in the accusation of Angelo he is planning, but this lie is very cruel indeed. The Duke is cruel, if only with souls and not bodies, but his cruelty is administered in the name of justice. He has a good reason for torturing her in this way as part of his taming of her. He has first gotten her used to dealing calmly with a certain carnality, and now he elicits from her a purely natural reaction to her

brother's death, tinged with some guilt about her own unwillingness
to act on his behalf. Revenge is for now her only motive, and she becomes utterly attached to her holy mentor and the ruler he serves.
Both will be replaced in her esteem by the Duke as duke.

Most of Act IV takes place in the dark prison, where the Duke, as
religious man, prepares his final rendering of justice, which will
take place in the light of day in the public place in Act V. In the prison
the Duke is at his most deceitful and Italianate—he claims to have
been sent on a mission by the Pope. He commands the Provost, using
the authority of the Duke's signs; in a parallel to his mission from the
Pope, he acts in the name of a higher power. He is loath to act directly
because he himself would appear to be partly responsible for the
abuses he is correcting, and he is arrogating to himself a form of justice
akin to that of Angelo. A significant part of the play is devoted to the
disproportion between reality and seeming in the exercise of rule and
justice. The Duke needs not only to resurrect the force of law but also
to mitigate the disproportion of which he has spoken. His problem as
a ruler, like Prospero's, is connected with a modesty about assuming
the false godlike proportions of rulers and a distaste for all the
hypocrisy surrounding those in high positions. This reticence is
heightened by all the scenes with Lucio, who calumniates the Duke to
the Duke, not knowing who he is. The comic delight of these scenes is
connected with justice, for the audience knows surely that Lucio will
repent of his loose tongue as soon as he knows whose face is hidden by
the friar's cowl. Unawares, Lucio tells the awful truth when he says,
"Cucullus non facit monachum," a cowl does not make a monk (V.i.261).
As Prospero adopted magic to right the situation, the Duke uses the
priest's deceits to do the same thing.

His prison is an interesting place where the treatment of the inmates is extremely gentle. The only death recorded is due to natural
causes. As already mentioned, Pompey is enlisted as deputy executioner for executions that never take place. He likes the job and remarks that executioners ask for pardon of their clients much more
often than do the whores to whom he has been the deputy in the past.
They were probably dealing out death just as liberally as do executioners. The prison makes Pompey feel right at home because it is now
populated with all the lowlifes who used to frequent the whorehouse.

Nothing very serious seems to be happening to them, and the only ones we actually see being consigned to the prison have been so only after repeated offenses. While there, the Duke saves Claudio, who has learned his lesson. He interviews the alleged murderer Barnardine, whose head he intended to send to Angelo in place of Claudio's. Barnardine refuses to die on that day because he is suffering from a hangover, and the Duke agrees that he is no more ready for death than for life. He first says that he will wait for Barnardine to be ready to die. Then the only clearly chance happening that occurs in the play is made known. A pirate who resembles Claudio much more than does Barnardine dies, and his head is dispatched to Angelo. In the end, Barnardine is pardoned by the Duke, probably because there is some doubt about whether he actually committed the murder of which he was accused. The tone of the prison is conveyed by the Provost, who says that Barnardine could easily have escaped but never had the energy to do so. This prison in no way confirms the harshness of the law that it is supposed to represent. The ghoulish sending of the head intended to deceive Angelo, and the lie, the same lie connected with the head, told to Isabella about her brother's death, seemings rather than realities, are the only harsh deeds that emanate from this prison.

Act V is the great affirmation of the Duke's policies and the public presentation of his refurbished position as dispenser of justice. He comes almost as a Messiah to satisfy the longing for justice on the part of the injured and to dispense punishment to the wrongdoers. All that has gone before, and particularly the subterranean activities of the disguised Duke in the prison, are the necessary preparations for his return to rule. The law requires much that is extralegal or even frankly illegal in order to be both just and applied. Shakespeare combines a Machiavellian critique of the law and of those who use it and abuse it with a classical, that is Platonic, Aristotelian, or Ciceronian, love of justice. The Duke is neither the dupe of the law nor a despiser of it.

He is met at the gates of the city in the public place by Isabella. Demanding redress from the Duke on whom she counts and who has asked for complaints, she is summarily clapped in prison for calumniating his minister of justice. This was extremely unpleasant for her and must be added to the list of things the Duke makes her undergo. One begins to pity her, in spite of her earlier stiff-necked self-righteousness. This scene mirrors the usual course of justice in states where the wronged are not believed in the face of the wrongdoers who are in the positions of respectability. The perpetual complaint against the law, articulated so powerfully by Thrasymachus in Plato's *Republic*, is that it is used by the rich and powerful to legitimize their aggrandizements.[7] This undermines men's confidence or hopes in the law. The final scene of *Measure for Measure* comically represents the realization of the human dream of the all-knowing and the all-powerful ruler or god who comes onto the scene to lift up the downtrodden and humiliate the arrogant. But it begins as a typical case of the disproportion between power and justice.

Isabella lies to the Duke, telling him that she acceded to the demands of Angelo in order to save her brother. Thus, she makes a public, if untrue, confession to the loss of her virginity. She is most probably wearing a religious novice's costume when she does so. In another sense, of course, she is vindicating herself before the public because she is claiming to have been willing to sacrifice herself for her brother's life. Finally, she is forced by Mariana's prayers to get on her knees and beg for Angelo's pardon. She explains that Angelo's career of crime began because of his being attracted to her. If she hadn't made such a big deal of it and had not placed such a high value on her virginity, Angelo would never have been corrupted.

Shakespeare in this play obviously tends to blame the sexual desires of males for most of the problems, and to pardon and to exculpate the women, but he also investigates the subtle mechanisms involved in the sexual relations between civilized, indeed overcivilized, human beings. He walks a narrow line between a legitimate concern and respect for the modesty of women and a sacralization of their virginity. In the three cases of offending males he judges in this scene, the Duke acts in favor of offended women in spite of the fact that they were apparently all consenting. The only exception is to be found in the treatment of Isabella.

As soon as Friar Lodowick is brought on the scene, with conflicting testimony about his character and reliability, the kind of conflicting testimony one finds so often in the exercise of human justice, the climax has been reached. His hood is ripped off him by Lucio, who has been the chief calumniator of both the friar and the Duke, a kind of chorus representing the shifting and dangerous moods of public opinion, and all the principals become aware that they are in the presence of a man who knows of their secret thoughts and doings and who can dispense superlegal justice to them. But it is Angelo, the doer of the only deed intentionally designed to harm others, who is most disarmed when he recognizes that he must meet his judgment day. He counted on a kind of Gygean invisibility to protect him from the consequences of his crimes, although his conscience distressed him with the possibility that there might be a divine observer. Now he finds himself in the presence of a human observer:

> O my dread lord,
> I should be guiltier than my guiltiness
> To think I can be undiscernible,
> When I perceive your Grace, like power divine,
> Hath looked upon my passes. (V.i.364–368)

The Duke appears as God to him, and the deepest guilt would be to believe that he will be unseen in his crimes. Men like Angelo, and in this respect there are a lot of them, must above all believe they are being seen by a higher power in order to remain just. The Duke gives Angelo and Lucio and many others the impression that he will always be spying them out in the secret crevices of their minds. The Duke's justice is speedily accomplished, and in all four cases before him the decision is for marriage. The Duke's policy is pro-family, with particular emphasis (the cases of Angelo and Lucio) on males taking responsibility for the children they made women bear. The Duke, unlike our moral reformers, who concentrate on peripheral issues like abortion, homosexuality, or pornography, goes to the heart of the problem. He looks to making and maintaining marriages. It is not, however, entirely an accident that these marriages look something like punishments.

The resolution of Angelo's case is the most curious of them all. The punishment of death, which the Duke first assigns and which is wished for by Angelo himself, is tempered by the clemency of the Duke, moved by the pleas of the two women. Mariana believes for a few moments that she must marry and become a widow on the same day, exactly the same kind of paradox she suffered for a day or two when she was both maiden and consummated wife. The sufferings of all other characters in this play seem to be fair, but it remains a mystery why Mariana must go through this torment, except as a means to the end of correcting Angelo. The Duke does test her in this way and confirms her implausible love of Angelo. She is to receive all his property, thus allowing her to realize the dream of many a widow. This would restore her to the situation that existed prior to her brother's death at sea and the loss of her dowry with him. The Duke provides her with the means to look for a better husband, but she will have none of it. Although the play's title is *Measure for Measure*, a version of the *lex talionis*, it might be, at least for Mariana, *All's Well That Ends Well*. The Duke presents a soft version of an eye for an eye: a threat of death for a threat of death, not a death for a death. However, Angelo did do a horrible thing, intending really to kill Claudio. Claudio was, of course, under sentence of death, undergoing the rigors of a law that was on the books. The punishment is indeed severe, but Angelo was appointed, at least for the benefit of the public, to apply such laws. His fault is breaking the promise he made to Isabella-Mariana, which is a business outside the law. His legal crime is using his power to force a woman to have intercourse with him. The Duke has used Angelo in both ways—to reinvigorate the law and to soften the moral severity of the judge. It is possible that the Duke believes Isabella's account of the reasons for Angelo's crimes and thinks there is better stuff in him that will come out after the fall.

The Duke's providence is the cause of Isabella's not being violated and Claudio's not being beheaded. He performs miracles. Isabella is impressed by his action but thinks he failed to save her brother. All he has offered is "the appeal to heaven," for the punishment of wrongdoers. At the very end, she recognizes that his providence deals with everything that is most dear to her. One of the most interesting aspects of the Duke's justice is that he leaves no one with the satisfactions of indignation, of getting back at offenders, or even of repenting for sins committed. Marriages, reunions with brothers, natural satisfactions, are what the Duke deals in. Escalus is praised and the provost rewarded. Lucio is compelled to marry a woman who has, according to Lucio's own admission, borne him a child that he has denied and whom he now calls a whore, so that he is to receive, as he says, a cuckold's horns in return for having made the Duke a duke (by pulling off the friar's cowl). Teaching men to accept responsibility for their children is part of this punishment of Lucio, but the primary reason is, as I have said, his disrespect for the Duke and his tales of the Duke's own sexual conduct. The two reasons are perhaps identical: respect for the Duke must be respect for the Duke's law in these essential matters.

Claudio is assigned the marriage that he claimed he wanted without any discussion of the dowry he was waiting for. Since we know that Mariana has no dowry, and Lucio's blushing bride surely had none, the Duke is removing from women the burden of providing money to husbands.

And now we come to the case of Isabella and the Duke. He proposes marriage, once prior to the miraculous coming to life of Claudio, and once after. We never hear her response, but his authority is such that we cannot doubt that she agreed. The Duke moves from the state of single man to the state of marriage, and he makes the whole population follow him in the move. This is a play that speaks almost not at all of love. It is full of sex and empty of eros. The kinds of marriage here ascend from Lucio's disgust, to Angelo's resignation and relief, to Claudio's easygoing satisfaction, to the Duke's apparent love. Shakespeare plays Jane Austen in giving everybody the kind of marriage he or she deserves. The Duke thinks he deserves the best. He has chosen a very attractive girl and has educated her before our eyes. She ends up with admiration for his wisdom and power, and gratitude for his having saved both her and her brother. He begins his marriage holding very good cards. He will need them because this is a woman very much with her own mind. Most of all, the Duke has robbed the convent of a promising sister to provide his bed with a delicious wife.

This last fact is the one that best teaches us about the spirit of the Duke's great reform. This is a terrible play in its threats, and a very sweet one in its results. The Duke understands effective law to be a delicate mixture of fear-producing force, wisdom, and, above all, natural inclination, producing as much happiness for individuals as human society admits of. He does not believe that sexual desire can express itself without limits in a decent society. He thinks sexual satisfaction is a good thing and that it does not take too much, unless there has been a total emancipation, to calm sexual desire sufficiently in the name of marriage. In the Holy Roman Empire we see a friar turning into a married ruler, a reform not unrelated to the Protestant reform. Everything he does is for the sake of natural satisfactions, in the first place, his own. Unlike his Enlightenment successors, he does not think that natural inclination is simply sufficient for the constitution of an orderly society, but he agrees in large measure with their aims.

Sexual education, the Duke agrees with Rousseau, is an essential part of citizenship education. The Duke, however, does not embark on a great transformation of man in order to overcome his divided-ness. He simply introduces fear into the sexual scheme of things. The sexual prying of authority is distasteful, but the Duke engages in it so that it will not have to be done again. And he underlines by this activ-ity that the sexual character of men is an essential component in their relation to the polity.

chapter four

TROILUS AND CRESSIDA

Troilus and Cressida, perhaps the bleakest of all Shakespeare's plays, presents itself as a wildly witty travesty of antiquity's greatest heroes. Shakespeare's message seems to be that heroes are not heroes, because they are either fools or knaves, and that love is a sham and deception. The atmosphere is very different from that of *Antony and Cleopatra,* so different that many interpreters can render the change intelligible only by supposing disappointments in love undergone by the Bard. Such explanations appeal to modern readers, who, under the persisting influence of Romanticism, understand writers as chroniclers of their own personal histories or their moods, sublime reproductions of the way most of us approach things. The notion that a writer overcomes his particular experience or feeling in the name of a more comprehensive and less personal view of things is rejected and treated as antipoetic, although this suggestion is enunciated by Shakespeare himself and discussed even in this play. It is more a commentary on ourselves that we take the autobiographical explanation as truth, when it is little better than an assertion, and an implausible one at that. We should at least consider that Shakespeare looks at the ancient heroes and love under different aspects in different plays and that each of the aspects is part of a total vision. Why should a man generally understood to be of such divine gifts not be able to discipline his thoughts? He may very well have used his moods to understand the psychology of the passions, that is, to reveal the human situation, not

---

All parenthetical citations in this chapter are to Shakespeare's *Troilus and Cressida,* ed. Kenneth Palmer, Arden Edition (1982; rpt. London: Routledge, 1989).

merely his personal experiences. The play, which actually exists and which we can keep before our eyes, has to be understood prior to our speculating about the poet's motives, which we really cannot know apart from their product, the play. Otherwise the unknowable becomes the basis for interpreting the knowable. These reflections are induced by reading the play itself, for it is most baffling. The high good humor, the outrageous anachronisms, and the ridiculing of a tradition that Shakespeare seems elsewhere to admire so highly, puzzle us. *Troilus and Cressida* contains very great poetry, but its form and its rhetorical character, including long speeches that could hardly be understood from the stage, seem to argue a dramatic failure. It is one of those plays that seem impossible to categorize as either comedy or tragedy.

Certainly if *Antony and Cleopatra* instills nostalgia in us, this play is the corrective of that dangerous sentiment. Nostalgia undermines the present in the name of the past, a historical moment that can never be reproduced, and ends up in empty snobbism. Here Shakespeare debunks the past, but it is not true that nothing is left standing. Nothing is left standing in the eyes of those who regard glory and love as the two greatest and most interesting human motives. But if, to put it bluntly, this is a play about wisdom, a thing neither understood nor desired by most people, then many of the play's formal difficulties disappear. One character, Ulysses, emerges, if in an understated way, triumphant. Shakespeare suggests in *Troilus and Cressida* that wisdom, austere and externally unattractive, is the one thing permanently available to man that is noble and choiceworthy. The difficulty Shakespeare has in presenting this theme is the old Platonic one: the lively and intense passions are what the imitative arts can depict, whereas the wise man (e.g., Socrates) has no important role on the stage that mirrors life. This is the same problem, in another guise, that Shakespeare grapples with in *The Tempest*, that is, how a wise man can be made interesting amid the passions, despite the popular lack of understanding of wisdom and distaste for it. Glory and love, always attractive and interesting, are central to *Troilus and Cressida*, but their splendor is dimmed by the corrosive of reason, and they become in the plot means to the ends of Ulysses. Just as Ulysses in Homer's *Iliad* is hardly a favorite character, Ulysses is not much liked in *Troilus and Cressida* and is very underrated by its critics. Prospero, the magician, can hold center stage. Ulysses, the intriguer and debunker, appears peripheral to the play's central action. But for a few choice viewers or readers he represents the consolation of philosophy in a dark world.

The characters in the play are very preoccupied with posterity's judgment and recognize that their glory depends upon poets. Shakespeare really gives it to them. The only person who comes out looking good in the popular eye is Troilus, and even he seems a bit silly. This play is written by an extremist who pulls no punches. Shakespeare chooses to represent the Trojans as much superior to the Greeks, a very different picture from that given by the evenhanded Homer. This allows Shakespeare to treat the victorious heroic tradition in an irreverent way. The Trojan men generally live up to their legends, idealists of honor, whereas the Greek heroes are painted in a most repulsive light, but one that reflects something of what they really were. The rulers are not wise, the heroes are not honorable, and there are no lovers among them. The presence of Ulysses helps to bring all of this out or makes it worse than it might ordinarily appear to be, but it is all too evident even without him, and Shakespeare's play would seem to correct a great historical error, the burden of which misleads men of later ages. It is Achilles, the hero of all heroes, who is most transformed, and Shakespeare thereby makes much more central what Plato hinted at in the *Republic*.[1]

This play inserts erotic motives behind the actions of the various heroes in a way that is not evident in Homer, but it follows and enhances the erotic motive alleged to have been at the root of the Trojan War. The struggle for the possession of Helen's beauty was supposed to explain or give sufficient reason for the great sufferings and heroic deeds of this war. The love of the beautiful can be considered a noble motive for great dedication and great sacrifices in a way that the quest for money or land cannot be. The Greeks and the Trojans elevated war by their ideals. *Troilus and Cressida* demotes the war by ridiculing its motives. This is exactly what Herodotus does at the beginning of his *History*.[2] He does so in order to put the Persian War in the place of the Trojan War as a truly noble war. Shakespeare, however, presents no such noble alternative and in that resembles Thucydides, who leaves understanding as the only satisfaction arising from the contemplation of the ugliness of political history. The opposition between Venus and Mars is underlined and undermined at the same time.

One of the peculiarities of the play is its turning the Greek and Trojan, especially the Trojan, warriors into knights who, in the great tradition of chivalry, have great ladies for whom they fight and whose combats are enclosed in high, ridiculous forms. In *Troilus and Cressida,* this reaches its peak with the combat between Hector and Ajax, where each falls over the other with terms of endearment and the enunciation of shared principles of honor. Not the slightest harm is done by either to the other. The background of this combat is senseless slaughter of both Greeks and Trojans. Thus the high principles, the gentlemanliness of the leading combatants, is ridiculed, and the ugliness of the war revealed. In reading this play, one cannot help being reminded of the First World War, in which so many died for slight or even nonexistent goals. During a large part of this war there were civil and formal relations between aristocratic French and German officers, beautifully captured in Jean Renoir's film *Grand Illusion.* The difference between Renoir and Shakespeare is that Renoir solemnly teaches us about the vanity of war whereas Shakespeare presents this picture with unfailing gaiety. Folly is a permanent feature of human existence. The playwright cannot change that and can at best offer us consolation in laughter and the insight laughter brings with it. Never does he sermonize. The spoof of Christian chivalry in the context of the Trojan War, inherited from Chaucer, permits Shakespeare also to raise the question of the motives of classical warriors.

We are introduced to the play in a scene where Troilus has chosen not to go to war today because he is love-moody. The war is treated as something one can participate in or not according to whether one feels like it that day. Erotic life is viewed from a double perspective, as a war between the sexes and as a much more pleasant way of spending one's time than fighting. This picks up on a theme mentioned, but not insisted on, in the *Iliad,* where Paris is spirited away from the battlefield by Aphrodite to the bed of Helen and is chided for his sport by the ever serious Hector. The opposition between the erotic life and the most serious activity of politics, war, is the central message of this first scene, but it is never forgotten that this war as a whole is fought for Helen, so that the toils of war are means to the end of peaceful enjoyment of beauty. This robs of its intrinsic nobility the heroic fighting of an Achilles, and if Helen is a whore, then its instrumental nobility also disappears, as does the dignity of love. This is what Ulysses' action in the play accomplishes. It will ultimately restore peace, but peace that is lived merely for the sake of life, without the glory of war or the grace of eros.

Most of the love talk in this play rings false, and at best reminds us of a Ginger Rogers–Fred Astaire romance. Pandarus, the go-between, has a superficial urbanity and is a big booster of sexual connections, as opposed to either marriages or grand loves à la Romeo and Juliet or Antony and Cleopatra, where no go-betweens are needed. He is a character reminiscent of Viennese light opera. All these associations to literary types who have nothing to do with Homer show something about the range of Shakespeare's understanding of kinds of relatedness among men and women. When I was young I saw Tyrone Guthrie's production of *Troilus and Cressida,* and all I remember about it is that he made the meeting between the Greek and Trojan heroes in Act IV into a cocktail party, and it played very well as such. Shakespeare shows us real love, acted out solo by Troilus; gallantry, described by Rousseau as a parody of love, a routine form of passion with the certainty of consummation, represented by Pandarus, Helen, and Paris; and simple looseness and whorishness, played by Cressida and Diomedes. Ulysses is the only one who has nothing to do with anything of this, although he is a shrewd observer of it.

After Troilus' earnest but sophomoric love talk in scene i, we get Cressida playing the perfect coquette, prior to her descent into wantonness, with Pandarus. Whatever our prejudices about the appropriate behavior for men and women, we see immediately that someone who talks like Cressida cannot be serious. She plays the game of not taking Troilus seriously, and comparing him unfavorably with the other Trojan heroes who pass across the stage and upon whom she comments to Pandarus. And she proves her ecumenism by asking how Troilus would compare with the Greek Achilles, thus giving us a harbinger of her later conduct. She is much too experienced with sexual acts and sexual organs to be thought to be in any way innocent, or to respect their deeper meaning and mysteriousness. With her, it all hangs out. The innocent Juliet desires with purity and awe; Cleopatra knows it all and is witness to the qualitative superiority of Antony in the act. When Pandarus asserts that Helen loves Troilus, Cressida responds, "Troilus will stand to the proof" (I.ii.131). Exclusivity is not within Cressida's ken, and she accepts with urbanity Troilus' presumed bodily movements when attended to by Helen. When Pandarus describes Troilus as a man of good nature and liberal education, Cressida remarks that these are the qualities of "a minced man; and then to be baked with no date in the pie, for then the man's date is out" (I.ii.261–

262). Date refers to Troilus' intimate parts. It is not that Cressida speaks frankly in a "pagan" style; it is that this is all common currency for her. Hers is a lustful statement of what we know as the sexual teachings of Masters and Johnson. When, at the end of scene ii, she has a soliloquy in which she professes her seriousness about Troilus, one recognizes that it is a very relative seriousness indeed. She explains her coyness as a means to ensure Troilus' seriousness. By experience or report, she knows that men are likely to despise what they get easily. She wants to appear difficult in order to maintain the upper hand after as well as before. She understands ordinary sexual relations to be a mere alternation of mastery and slavery. The disguising of her desires is only the better to satisfy them. This is a parody of a serious woman's reflections on her vulnerability. For her it is only an exercise in sexual economics. How different she is from Juliet, who recognizes the risk in giving herself so frankly, but accepts it. The acquisition of Troilus is merely an act of vanity. If she were to lose him, she would suffer from wounded pride, but not very much, because there are others where he came from.

The shift from Troy to the Greek camp in Act I, scene iii, is brutal. The Greek side is utterly unerotic, although there is a certain amount of brutish sex of the kind well known in armies. Here one finds a public debate about what is going wrong in the war. There are two ridiculous speeches, formal orations full of the commonplaces of public moral discourse, one by the king of kings, the shepherd of the host, Agamemnon, the other by his supporter and wise counselor, the aged Nestor (I.iii.1–54). These speeches are meant to hearten the host, but they are platitudes worthy of a current State of the Union address and could not arouse anyone. To a certain extent, they are coverups for the incompetence of the leaders. The difficulty, as is well known from the *Iliad,* is that Achilles is quarreling with the generals and keeping to his tent. But this is not mentioned by the speakers, who respond to the low morale in the army by explaining that the war is taking so long and costing so many men because of its place in the providential scheme of things. According to Agamemnon, this is Jove's way of testing the Greeks and showing what they are. Both speakers base themselves on a Stoic public morality, which, in distinguishing between virtue and fortune, makes human worth depend on the former while it holds out against the blows of the latter. True happiness is virtue, and the virtuous man will be happy and most himself when fortune is most hostile and he holds out against it. Dumb luck can procure all kinds of good things, including victory, but only those who have earned these things are truly admirable. It is an affront to human nature to say that what most counts depends on mere accident and not on the qualities of men. Therefore the current adversity is a blessing in disguise that will ensure the glory of the Greeks. Both Agamemnon and Nestor cheat a bit, probably unconsciously, in asserting that virtue is everything and then insisting that virtue will be rewarded by victory. Virtue should be its own reward, but this can never be believed by the multitude. Agamemnon and Nestor are simply haranguing the crowd in the hope that its members will learn patience.

Neither Agamemnon nor Nestor suggests that fortune can be conquered. It must be endured. Virtuous conduct is absolute and cannot alter itself to circumstances. There is in this an element of the noble classical teaching about what men must learn to live with, as opposed to modern teachings, which insist that they must be chameleons in thrall to chance. But this argument can easily turn into an excuse for idleness or stupidity. Machiavelli calls for the conquest of fortune in order to combat such passivity, which cripples the statesman's prudence and action. Although Machiavelli's generalization that what men call fortune is only the result of lack of foresight is not simply correct, there is much to it, and Ulysses' speech and the action later founded upon it are a page out of Machiavelli's book (I.iii.54–137).[3] His explanation of the problem the Greeks face amounts to an indictment of Agamemnon's inattention or incompetence, although he does not insist on making this conclusion public. Ulysses' rhetorical problem is that he has to persuade imprudent or unwise rulers of the proper course to follow, and they need not obey him as he must obey them, since his prudence or wisdom has no status in the order of things. Ulysses begins by praising Agamemnon for the position he holds and Nestor for his age. Agamemnon is king of kings because he is king of kings. There is no good reason for it. He was simply born to the position and the position must be respected. Nestor is respected for his age, since in traditional societies at least, age, simply because it is age, has authority. Reverence for the ancestral gives power, and the younger and wiser Ulysses must flatter Nestor. It is a rare thing when wisdom can peep through these thickets into the light of day, and a consummate rhetorician like Ulysses must present its case. He succeeds by making Agamemnon and Nestor indignant that their positions are being called into question by Achilles. Ulysses' wise plans succeed because he makes them appeal to the unwise passions of his hierarchical superiors.

And it is just the overturning of this rank order of things that Ulysses blames for the current discontents. Men do not obey their superiors. Why not? Because those superiors are incompetent and do not know how to control their inferiors. Actually, this means that the superiors are only conventionally superior. Ulysses, who knows how to right the situation and, in spite of the handicaps of his position, succeeds in doing so, is the only natural ruler on the scene. But natural rulers are not real rulers.

Ulysses dresses up his proposals in cosmic clothing. There is an order in all things, beginning with the heavens themselves, of which the human orders are a part. When priority is not observed, the whole falls into chaos. The good for eve\ything is connected with this order of ruling and being ruled. This is a statement of the Great Chain of Being, about which so much nonsense has been written and which is supposed to have provided men with moral security prior to the Enlightenment. It is another one of those organic explanations of political relations that tell us about the way things ought to be but that are in fact only ideologies. Ulysses ridicules this cosmology as it is applied to human things. It is not unlike the divine order of things relied on by Richard II, which exempts him from having to accept the responsibilities of ruling.[4] The beehive is a favorite analogy to the political order, and Ulysses uses it. But in beehives nobody has to tell the workers what they must do or who the ruler of the hive is. There are no bees sulking in their tents. One might say that the hive is the model for the way things ought to be, but this is made questionable by the fact that nature does not produce human communities in the way that it does beehives. Human communities are much more a product of force and fraud exercised by rulers. Ulysses intentionally leaves his audience in some confusion as to whether the cosmic order itself has good and bad elements that require a cosmic ruler to control them or whether that order is permanent with all the parts ultimately contributing to a common good. This confusion has something to do with events such as killer storms that are not liked by human beings and seem to indicate

disorder in the nature of things. If there were such disorder, men's rebelliousness and despair would have some justification. But if such
storms are part of the good of the whole, then that whole is not necessarily friendly to human wishes or aspirations.

This beautiful cosmic picture amounts only to an indictment of
the actual rulers. Ulysses presents high moral grounds, and immediately turns to a low and dishonest conspiracy to institute the proper
relations of ruling and being ruled. Ulysses' speeches must be interpreted in the light of his deeds, and vice versa, for what appear to be
low deeds become noble ones when understood in the light of the public good. This is Machiavelli's teaching.

Ulysses makes it clear that appetite, potentially "an universal
wolf" (I.iii.121), must be subjected to power rather than allowed to
make power its tool. This subjection comes from human action, not
natural inclination. After his pompous elucidation of their difficulty,
which has nothing to do with the fortune blamed by Agamemnon and
Nestor, Ulysses gets down to cases and blames the couple, Achilles
and Patroclus, as the source of rottenness in the state. This play, as I
have said, ridicules almost all Greek things, and one of those well-
known Greek things was pederasty. In this play, everyone takes
Achilles and Patroclus to be sexually involved. The word "lovers"
would be something of an overstatement, although these days the
word is almost always an overstatement. This kind of sexual relation
has none of the chivalry that one finds in the other kinds of connection
in the play. It is treated as an expression of pride and factiousness (not
particularly of lustfulness). This relationship will ultimately be politically useful, when Patroclus' death draws Achilles back into battle.
The ancient view that couples of male lovers could be the source of
conspiracy to overthrow tyranny, as in the case of Harmodius and
Aristogeiton,[5] is not utterly rejected, if in any sense Agamemnon can
be considered a tyrant.

Ulysses takes a very curious tack in describing the seditious speech
of Achilles and Patroclus. He says Patroclus calls his jests "imitation."
Ulysses appears to think that to call such subversive stuff imitation is
a slander of imitation. Patroclus means by imitation what Aristotle
means in the *Poetics*.[6] Patroclus is an artist whose art is subversive. If
one looks closely at what Ulysses tells us about these "imitations,"
they are perfect representations of what we actually see in Agamemnon and Nestor—Agamemnon a blowhard, Nestor a doddering old

fool. Patroclus does in bed with Achilles what Shakespeare does on the stage:

> With him Patroclus
> Upon a lazy bed the livelong day
> Breaks scurril jests,
> And with ridiculous and awkward action,
> Which, slanderer, he imitation calls,
> He pageants us. (I.iii.146–151)

Shakespeare's understanding of imitation can help to enrich the stiff modern interpretations of that term. Here the imitator produces a painting of a natural understanding of the political scenery, a painting that is subversive of the official understanding. The imitator imitates nature, as opposed to convention, and that is not so simple and stupid an activity as is often thought. Ulysses pretends to want to suppress, as do all tyrants in such cases, the mockery by Achilles' boyfriend, who thus amuses his senior partner. However, Ulysses silently but powerfully promotes an appreciation of the Greek leaders similar to Patroclus'. There is no doubt that imitation can be dangerous as well as salutary for civic morals. Only the loose and liberated are capable of such imitative art. The imitations are liberating, except for the fact that the audience, in this case Achilles, also needs imitations that would not simply flatter it. The imitator is limited by the nature of his audience, and that is indeed a problem for art, a problem that only the greatest of poets can solve. All the advantages and disadvantages of imitation as discussed by Plato are discussed in this passage. Shakespeare does for us, concerning all of what is handed down to us from Greece, what Patroclus does for Achilles concerning Agamemnon and Nestor.

The trouble with Achilles, according to Ulysses, is that he is all brawn and no brains. The heroes "count wisdom as no member of the war" (I.iii.198). They esteem only the battering ram and not the one who built it or the reason that guided the builder. This thought confirms the difficulty of Ulysses' position, which we have already noted. Unfortunately, poetry itself tends to share this point of view. It celebrates the glorious deeds of the heroes and not what does or should lie behind them. Strength and rage are made to seem to be the summit of human virtue and to contain within them all the other qualities. This is the reason why Ulysses, the wisest of the Greeks, must appear to be a very secondary character in the *Iliad,* and not a very sympathetic one at that. To repeat, wisdom is not in itself attractive. But Shakespeare in *Troilus and Cressida* brutally corrects the poetic preference for the warrior.

The Greek council is interrupted by the arrival of Aeneas, another of the great Trojan romantics. He is there to propose single combat between Hector and any of the Greeks who is willing to face him. It is a challenge for lovers who assert the superiority in beauty and chastity of their beloveds over those of their opponents. Aeneas appears to believe in this nonsense, whereas it is utterly alien to the Greeks. It is pride in women that leads knights to fight. Rousseau said that men no longer dueled because they no longer believed in the chastity of women or its importance.[7] Aeneas is a man of the old order. Of course, there is a political intention underlying this challenge, because the Trojans expect Achilles to take it up and thus, perhaps, in this relatively cheap way, to end the war.

Aeneas' words bring out everything that is most ridiculous in Agamemnon and Nestor. Agamemnon assures Aeneas that some of his soldiers are lovers and hence will respond to the challenge, but promises, if there are none, he will do it himself. He does not say with whom he is in love. Clytemnestra is not mentioned. Nestor goes Agamemnon one better and declares himself ready to confront Hector, asserting that his dead wife is more beautiful than Hector's grandmother. This is rendered all the more hilarious by Patroclus' imitation of Nestor with palsied hand trying to put on a suit of armor. Aeneas responds to this with "Now heavens forfend such scarcity of youth." To which Ulysses, showing his own brand of humor, appends the single word "Amen" (I.iii.301–302).

As Aeneas goes off with Agamemnon for ceremonial visits in the Greek camp, Ulysses uses the occasion to speak to Nestor, who will presumably speak to Agamemnon, about the scheme he has conceived, connected with this challenge, to correct the chaos caused by Achilles. Simply, it is to set up a crooked lottery for the choice of the Greek combatant. The result of this lottery, which will appear to be chance but is actually controlled by Ulysses, will be that Ajax will go rather than Achilles. The defeat of Ajax would not, with Achilles still in reserve, completely dishearten the Greeks. If Ajax wins, so much the better. But in any case, Achilles will be humiliated and brought back into the order of things by the loss of reputation. Ulysses' shrewd management of this scheme is the theme of the rest of the play.

The meeting of the Greek notables is paralleled by a meeting of the Trojan notables (II.ii) that, in its way, is a real deliberation about the purposes and conduct of the war. It all turns on Helen. Old Priam has received a communication from Nestor saying that the war can be ended simply by the return of Helen and that there will be no further demands. Priam is clearly inclined to meet Nestor's demand because he grieves for the terrible losses incurred during this war and fears for the very existence of Troy. The debate is initiated by the noble and decent Hector, who argues in favor of peace. He knows that no one can doubt his courage as a warrior, so he can confidently, without fear of accusation as a coward, take the side of ending the war on grounds of compassion. He concludes his first speech by saying that reason is on his side, and the entire debate becomes a disputation about the status of reason. This is, to say the least, an unusually theoretical, even academic, dispute in a play, especially a Shakespearean play. Of course, Shakespeare is not a crudely didactic writer who uses the stage as a platform for the direct propagation of his views. The arguments are a part of the action and are incomprehensible except in relation to the characters of those who enunciate them. They are opinions suitable to the individuals and teach us something about their dominant passions, which ultimately win out against any argumentation.

Hector's primary antagonist in the debate is the idealistic Troilus. He is unhesitating and equates fear and reason. No reason can be put in the scale to counterbalance the worth and honor of his father, the king. Reason is nothing against such "infinite" proportions. When he is chided by his older brother Helenus for being empty of reason, Troilus launches into a passionate attack on reason, which he identifies, like many of our contemporary men and women, with the mere calculating arm of self-preservation, which sees in glory only vanity. He stands foursquare for the noble and the splendid and seems certain that they cannot defend themselves against reason, if reason is credited. Reason cannot prove that the sacrifice of life in defense of a woman's honor or for the common good is preferable to safety and comfort:

> if we talk of reason,
> Let's shut our gates and sleep: manhood and honour
> Should have hare hearts, would they but fat their thoughts
> With this cramm'd reason: reason and respect
> Make livers pale, and lustihood deject. (II.ii.46–50)

It is almost as though Troilus and Shakespeare had read Hobbes, who was to write the *Leviathan* fifty years later, not to say thousands of years later. Troilus' position has just one weakness: he must use reason in his attack on reason, and this fact heightens the vulnerability of the position he enunciates.

Hector argues, in keeping with Troilus' description of the use of reason, that Helen is not worth the cost of keeping her, which forces Troilus into the position of saying that a thing is worth whatever it is valued at, that value is only subjective, a thing of men's imagination or fancy. This permits Hector to respond that esteeming must be related to the nature of what is esteemed if it is not to be mere folly: "'Tis mad idolatry / To make the service greater than the god" (II.ii.57–58). This gives Troilus the occasion to make his strongest point. We do not turn back to the merchant the silk we purchased from him when it is soiled. A wife no longer attractive is not thrown away. We make commitments, and we are supposed to stick by them. Here Troilus is closest to common opinion, and what he says is a truism, the logical extension of which is sticking by the Trojan decision to kidnap Helen in the first place. However, it is only an argument from common opinion, and one can very well sympathize with the desire to exchange old silks or old wives for new ones. Otherwise, one would have to agree with Troilus that the value of things is determined simply by our act of valuing them, and morality would be reduced to keeping one's promises not because they have a good result but merely because they are one's promises. This is the morality of Cephalus in the *Republic*. Reason most certainly challenges and tends to undermine the convictions that underlie ordinary morality. Troilus is a very moral man, and one can make no headway in getting him to doubt the desirability of being so. This is why he trusts Cressida. Ulysses is going to fix that for him, and thus destroy Troilus' dangerous idealism. This play treats reasonableness as a bleak thing, while casting in its lot with it.

The sham of rational debate is rudely interrupted by Cassandra's cries and her prophecies of doom for the Trojans. The conclusion of the debate, which is that the Trojans should stick by their guns no matter what, is heightened by Cassandra's reminder that this conclusion will bring about the disaster of Troy. Troilus' immediate response to her intervention is that the justness of acts is not determined by this or that outcome. Justice is an absolute. He is seconded by Paris, who understandably wants to keep Helen and use Troy and the Trojans to enable him to do so, unlike Hector and Troilus, who are disinterested. Priam intervenes to point out Paris' evident self-interest and thus to discredit his argument. Then, in one of the strangest and most hilarious moments in this play, Hector turns to Aristotle's authority to support his position (II.ii.167). Some interpreters have said that Shakespeare probably did not know that Aristotle came hundreds of years after Homer; they provide a counterpoint almost as funny as this scene is in itself. This entire deliberation is utterly implausible. When did heroes of any kind sit around and discuss first principles, let alone use philosophic texts to support their positions? Heroes are incarnate first principles that need no discussion. The very reflection on the status of heroic action undermines such action. It is only in the light of such reflection that you can have a strumpety Helen presented as the face "that launched a thousand ships."

The ultimate cause of the comic oddness of this play is the tension between heroic naïveté and reason. The intermediary between the two poles is constituted by the sexual nature of women. Hector points out that Paris and Troilus would not have been permitted by Aristotle to engage in serious moral deliberation. They can use words very well, but the proper use of words is connected to moral character. The young are too much under the sway of the passions to weigh those passions. The two passions that most affect young people, according to Hector's Aristotle, are pleasure and revenge. Paris seems to be more motivated by pleasure and Troilus by revenge, although this is not to say that Troilus' high-minded expectation of pleasure from love does not play a role in his arguments. Revenge is a passion closely allied to love of justice and is aroused by infractions of justice. Without its activity in the soul, justice would go unarmed. Perhaps the connection between pleasure and revenge has to do with protection of one's wife. Ulysses, confirming this interpretation, describes Troilus to Agamemnon as being:

Manly as Hector, but more dangerous;
For Hector in his blaze of wrath subscribes

> To tender objects, but he in heat of action
> Is more vindicative than jealous love. (IV.v.104–107)

These descriptions reflect a Platonic or Aristotelian tripartite division of the soul into appetite, anger, and reason. Having taken this scholastic high ground, Hector is able to argue on the basis of nature, the grounds of natural right to property. Helen was Menelaus' property and is therefore owed to him. It is a law of nature. The Trojans are breaking the laws of nature, and here Hector makes a sophisticated distinction between the laws of nature and the laws of nations (the *ius naturae* and the *ius gentium*). He concludes, "Hector's opinion / Is this in way of truth" (II.ii.189–190).

But, in an absolutely astounding and unexpected peripety, Hector chooses another way than that of the truth. After piling up good reason on good reason, he says, "Yet ne'ertheless. . ." His resolution is to keep Helen for the sake of all of their dignities. Thus he seals the doom of all of them. One could not present a starker picture of the contrariety of reason and heroic action. He reaches a conclusion without any arguments that have led to it. Shakespeare paints the folly of heroic choice, choice not preceded by deliberation, as vigorously as possible. Troilus, overjoyed by Hector's flip-flop, explains it by Hector's love of glory. The charming, thrilling love of glory is the villain of this play, and it works, in different ways, in both Hector and Achilles. No explaining it, but the heroes are distinguished above all other men by choosing glory over life. To put it in Nietzschean terms, here the noble man's instinct carries the day over slavish reason. Tragedy is somehow premised on the superiority of that instinct, and this is why *Troilus and Cressida* is not a tragedy. It ridicules, more or less brutally, the effect of that passion on men individually and on politics generally. Shakespeare does this in many other places, in particular in his portrait of Hotspur, the noble opponent of the cold and calculating Hal. No wonder that Ulysses, the bearer of the bad news about glory, is not very attractive to audiences who have a preference for the heroic. Socrates knows this and tries, ridiculously, in Plato's *Apology of Socrates,* to identify himself with the hero Achilles, who is the opposite of what he himself stands for.[8] This prejudice against reason explains why Ulysses' primary role in *Troilus and Cressida* is so often misunderstood by critics. The choice, as it presents itself to the popular imagination, is between dull, ignoble reasonableness and enspirit-

ing deeds performed for the sake of the beautiful, whether one understands the word "beautiful" with respect to women of fair form or to
glory.

These characteristics of heroic men are displayed in a much
harsher light in the Greek camp (II.iii). Thersites, the low expression of the grievances of the vulgar against the alleged persecu-
tions of the nobles, is transformed in this play into a fool in the medieval tradition, a clown who amuses kings and courts and has a right
to say all the things nobody else is permitted to say because he does so
in an amusing way and is not supposed to be taken seriously. He plays
a role akin to that of Patroclus as described by Ulysses and resembles
Shakespeare himself in his use of comedy. Thersites is an extreme of
foul-mouthed destructiveness. He describes himself as related to the
devil's envy. He is as low a character as one can imagine, and mad envy
of greatness is surely his motive. But for precisely this reason, he is
able to seek out the weaknesses of the great to whom he is intimately
connected and by whom he is persecuted. Mostly, his theme is the lack
of self-knowledge of the heroes in a play very much devoted to the
problem of self-knowledge.

Vanity is the great deceiver in telling us that we are what we are not
and making us dependent on public opinion. The exchanges between
Thersites and Ajax and Achilles reveal their pathological vanity.
Thersites tells them that they are more fools than he is, and he makes
it clear that Ajax is stupid and Achilles not too bright. They are
needed to beat down the Trojans and are given an opinion of themselves that identifies their dumb physical prowess with all the qualifications of the noble and the good. Thersites tells them they are
merely instruments manipulated by Ulysses and Agamemnon, although they think they are ends in themselves. These observations
made in such distasteful ways by Thersites are confirmed in deed on
the stage as Ulysses builds up Ajax's ego at the expense of Achilles.
Achilles has reached such a summit of sensitivity to his position that
his palate can no longer tolerate any nourishment other than that intended for the gods. Ajax's rivalry, his lust to equal or outdo Achilles,
makes him into the dupe of dupes. One sees him inflating like a bal-
loon as Ulysses pumps him up vis-à-vis Achilles. The comedy is very
broad indeed as Ajax claims that he cannot understand what vanity is

at the same time as he is, before our eyes, becoming the very exemplar of that vice.

The leading passions of Troilus and Achilles come to a climax in Act III, scenes ii and iii. In scene ii, Troilus and Cressida get together, make their declarations, and go off to their consummation. Troilus' speeches are beautiful and trusting, Cressida's coquettish. Pandarus brokers the whole thing with prurient attentiveness. There is no talk of marriage. The couple meet furtively, but *à la française*, without shame, and a rather large public is aware of what Pandarus has arranged. This situation heightens one's sense of Troilus' naive attachment to love. He seems to be utterly unaware of the circumstances, which indicate erotic levity on the part of Cressida. Troy is not like the Vienna of *Measure for Measure*. Troilus' father has been a solidly married man, and so is his brother Hector. But the moment is sufficient to satisfy expectations of eternity. Cressida complains when Troilus is about to go in the morning that all men leave too soon, not a remark made by an innocent. The scene ends with each of the three parties affirming his or her fidelity and predicting with confidence how posterity will view them. Troilus says that his name will be synonymous with truth; all men will say, "As true as Troilus." Cressida, strengthening her affirmation of her truthfulness, actually qualifies it by predicting that if she were to be false (a possibility in his own case that Troilus never even considered), her name will be idiomatic in "as false as Cressid." Pandarus casts Cressida's suggestion in a more neutral form and says, "If ever you prove false one to another," but then he accepts that it would be Cressida who would do the betraying: "let all constant men be Troiluses, all false women Cressids, and all brokers—between Pandars" (III.ii.180–202). Pandarus turns this into a prayer to which all say amen. It is a prayer that history has fulfilled, largely due to Chaucer and Shakespeare. The formula leaves Troilus as the only true person. And this is what the play teaches us. The question remains whether such unfounded idealism is simply admirable.

Act III, scene iii details Ulysses' corruption of Achilles. It is in some aspects one of the most shocking deeds in all of Shakespeare, for it leads directly to the murder of Hector by an Achilles who no longer has any concern for nobility. Only if this deed serves a greater good can there be any justification of it. Ulysses has, in the best tradition of rhetoric, prepared Achilles to hear him. He has done so by engineering Ajax's choice as the Greek representative in the knightly combat and by orchestrating the snub of Achilles by the Greek chieftains. Achilles is confused and distressed and seeks out Ulysses on his own. He needs Ulysses and wants clarification. He is now ready to be instructed, although he does not expect what he is going to get. Achilles finds Ulysses reading. What an extraordinary conceit, a Homeric hero reading! And he is from all evidence reading *Alcibiades I*. This encounter reminds one of the procedure of Socrates. In general, Socrates attracts the students to him by engaging their vanity. They look for a kind of support from him, and he takes them on a long ride into unknown terrain to which they are receptive because of their need. No self-satisfied man is open to Socratic seduction. The first thing he does is to destroy that self-satisfaction. Socrates uses vanity while ridiculing it and attempting to destroy it. He furthers the Delphic command, "Know thyself," and points out that vanity is the great enemy to self-knowledge and the substitute for it. These students need Socrates for this moment because he gives the impression that only he can help them regain their loss of self-assurance.

Ulysses says that the writer he is reading claims that a man cannot "boast to have that which he hath" (III.iii.98) except by mirror-like reflection in others that returns his virtues to himself. There is a critical ambiguity here in that *boast* usually has the negative implication of an attempt to mislead others, although it appears to mean here merely a claim. Moreover, the formula leaves it unclear whether the man who does not possess such a mirror actually has his virtues nevertheless and is only unconscious of them, or whether the virtues are actually dependent upon being reflected in this way. Achilles is ultimately persuaded that the distinction is an empty one and that the virtues exist only in the reputation for them.

Achilles shows himself to be aware of this literature by actually quoting the sense of Socrates' observation in *Alcibiades I*:

> nor doth the eye itself,
> That most pure spirit of sense, behold itself,
> Not going from itself; but eye to eye oppos'd
> Salutes each other with each other's form;

> For speculation turns not to itself
> Till it hath travell'd and is mirror'd there
> Where it may see itself. This is not strange at all.
> (III.iii.105–111)[9]

Achilles knows the *Alcibiades I* passage but has never been perplexed by it. Ulysses makes understanding it interesting for Achilles while perverting it. He leads Achilles into believing that what counts most or even exclusively is the image projected back on himself by the mirror and not the reality that is projected into it. Achilles was, up to this point, not a very appealing fellow, but he did have a salutary belief that he deserved his reputation because of his virtues. Such a man always remains a bit unsure whether the reputation for virtue is what is most important for him or whether virtue is its own reward, with reputation simply being a superadded pleasure. Aristotle discusses this question with great delicacy in the *Nicomachean Ethics* in the passage where he presents the proud man who claims great honors and deserves them. Such a man must have a certain contempt for honors, both because they come from individuals who are not his equals and hence not valid underwriters of his claims, and because virtue ought to be for its own sake.[10] There is in this description a fissure in the proud man's character that is important for the one who wishes to understand but on which it is imprudent to put too much stress, for fear that that character will split apart. This is the problem with the morality of the public man. Ulysses does put such stress on this historic model of the proud man and leads Achilles down the Machiavellian path that reputation for virtue is virtue, and that any means, fair or foul, are appropriate to getting that reputation. The plausibility of this conviction is attested to by the fact that Achilles kills Hector in the most ignoble way and gets perhaps the most brilliant reputation of any man in history by means of Homer's celebration of his deed. Shakespeare helps to correct this poetic abuse, but his correction does not lead in the direction of restoring the love of the kind of virtue professed by men like Achilles.

Ulysses speaks the best poetry in the play in the service of persuading Achilles of this terrible conclusion:

> Time hath, my lord, a wallet at his back
> Wherein he puts alms for oblivion,

A great-siz'd monster of ingratitudes.
Those scraps are good deeds past, which are devour'd
As fast as they are made, forgot as soon
As done. (III.iii.145–150)

These are truths, ugly truths, but truths. They are founded on Machiavelli's observations about gratitude and the bad character of men at large. Machiavelli suggests that the only way to deal with ingratitude is to keep men absolutely dependent on you so that your benefactions will never be in the past.[11] Of course, the critique of gratitude could very well lead to an abandonment of concern with public opinion altogether. This lack of concern for esteem would mean, however, a turn to private life or perhaps even to solitude, a position that at first blush would seem to diminish the scope of man and carries with it its own problems. Ulysses would seem to have drawn a similar conclusion from his analysis of the problem of fame. But he also knows perfectly well that there is a kind of man who has such a hunger for fame that all the critiques in the world fail to convince him. Such a man is Achilles, and the critique has the effect only of severing virtue from glory and making glory the only end. This is, not too surprisingly, the ultimate though unintended effect of Socrates' efforts in *Alcibiades I*. Socrates is dealing in Alcibiades with another loose cannon. His comparison of the eye of another with the soul of another is intended to make Alcibiades care about Socrates' opinion. He is trying to persuade Alcibiades to seek self-knowledge in company with a philosopher. But he also knows that Alcibiades is another man with the political hunger who turns to the city for the confirmation of his self. Alcibiades remains attached to Socrates but, at best, only halfway. Socrates ruins him by releasing him from the constraints that unconsciousness of moral ambiguity would have exercised over him and by reducing the dignity in his own eyes of the public acclaim that he so avidly seeks. Alcibiades clearly imitated Achilles, as did all men of heroic ambition, from Alexander to Caesar to Napoleon, whereas the Homeric hero to whom Socrates was regularly likened was Ulysses/Odysseus. Shakespeare presents Ulysses and Achilles imitating Socrates and Alcibiades who imitated Ulysses and Achilles.

Ulysses' point is seconded, in as touching an expression of affection as one finds on the Greek side, by Patroclus, who uses the epithet "sweet" in addressing Achilles. He tells Achilles that he, Patroclus, considers himself responsible for Achilles' loss of reputation, his affection for Patroclus having effeminated him (III.iii.215–224).

At the end of Ulysses' instruction of Achilles, he says that it was known that Achilles was keeping apart from the war because he was carrying on an affair with a Trojan princess. Achilles' motives in this play are unclear. The quarrel with Agamemnon over Briseis is not mentioned in the play, and Achilles' sulking is earlier attributed by Ulysses to his unwillingness to respect the rank order of things. Here Ulysses attributes it to a kind of treasonable connection across the lines of war, one that suits the medieval chivalry anachronistically connected with the Trojan heroes in particular. Ulysses reveals that the Greek intelligence system has knowledge of Achilles' secret deeds. He does this to show that the state is everywhere and one cannot hope to avoid its gaze. This love affair plays only a tiny role in the plot, and the death of Patroclus extinguishes it completely. Ulysses' instruction makes Achilles into a monster of glory, acquired by the reputation for virtuous deeds, not by virtue. It also shows him that his glory will have to be won in the context of the power of the Greek community. Ulysses liberates Achilles from moral concern and lowers his godlike pretensions.

Achilles' immediate response is an arousal of lust, to kill Hector. This is Achilles' authentic passion.

> I have a woman's longing,
> An appetite that I am sick withal,
> To see great Hector in his weeds of peace. (III.iii.236–238)

Act IV is devoted to bringing the two great couples—Troilus and Cressida, and Achilles and Hector—together in the same action. They represent the two interesting motives in this play, love and glory, and they both are debunked by Ulysses. War, in its unerotic necessity, separates Troilus and Cressida. Her father, Calchas the soothsayer, has defected to the Greeks and wants his daughter back with him. *Raison d'état* dictates an exchange of the girl for the hero Antenor. All the seamy sides of a Parisian-style erotic intrigue are again played out. It so happens that Troilus is, at the moment when Cressida must be exchanged, in a compromising position at her place. These are all men of the world, and they get Troilus out without a public scandal. It is always the comedy of this play that Troilus is faithful and wildly romantic in settings and with kinds of persons more appropriate to erotic farces. Troilus' farewell exhortations to Cressida are truly enchanting, whereas her responses are only coy (IV.iv.12–137). His potential jealousy of her is of the noble kind: he fears the Greeks will be more attractive than he is and immediately confronts the insolent Diomedes, who is sent to take possession of Cressida, and who taunts Troilus with threats of fooling around with his beloved.

In scene v both Cressida and Hector are seen among the Greeks. The supposedly heartbroken Cressida is liked by all the Greek heroes, with a single exception, Ulysses. The Greeks are full of prurient interest; she loves the whole thing and seasons it with ridicule of Menelaus, who, according to Pierre Bayle, was "the most debonair cuckold of antiquity."[12] This kissing feast is promoted by Ulysses. He gets her to ask him to kiss her, and then refuses her request.

ULYSSES: I do desire it.
CRESSIDA: Why, beg two.
ULYSSES: Why then, for Venus' sake, give me a kiss
    When Helen is a maid again, and his.
CRESSIDA: I am your debtor; claim it when 'tis due.
ULYSSES: Never's my day, and then a kiss of you. (IV.v.48–52)

Ulysses, avid to discredit the romantic motives, has orchestrated this little scene, and then humiliates Cressida by his refusal. Ulysses, just as he is the only one with a general awareness of the whole situation and with plans to change it, is a perfect reader of souls and their characters. His implicit and explicit opinions of Agamemnon, Nestor, Achilles, Hector, and Troilus are always perfectly on the mark. When Cressida exits, Ulysses makes a moralistic speech for the benefit of everyone there about Cressida's evident and disgusting sluttishness.

Then arrives the always gentle and enthusiastic Hector. He engages in all the formulas of knightly politeness, in which he actually believes. Aeneas speaks to Achilles of Hector's politeness and tells him that Hector cannot harm the foolish Ajax because Ajax is half Trojan. Achilles, continuing his erotic language about death, says, "A maiden battle, then?" (IV.v.87). Only the entry of the sword into the body interests him. The blurring of natural and historical differences, so characteristic of this play, makes what should be a climactic fight to the death between the two chosen representatives of the warring sides into a ceremonial gesture between chivalrous knights bound by blood without intention of doing harm. The great fight lasts only a second, a bit like the last trial by combat in *Richard II*.[13] It turns into a pageant with the exchange of the most exquisite compliments. The Greeks are perfect hypocrites in all this; Hector is a monster of sincerity.

As Ulysses has just dispelled the shadows of romantic illusion surrounding Cressida, Achilles chills us with his brutality, rendered much more extreme by the atmosphere of chivalric gentility in war. He comes in and looks at Hector as a butcher looks at a cow. Without any adornment he wonders how he will slaughter Hector, where on his body he will make the perforation out of which his spirit will fly, how he will dismember him. This is a rhetoric to which a Hector is unprepared to respond.

Act V is devoted to Cressida's infidelity to Troilus and to Hector's death. The first of these is the darkest of the dark scenes in *Troilus and Cressida*. Ulysses, fully aware of what is going on at Calchas' tent, takes Troilus to it and gives him "ocular proof" of Cressida's betrayal. Ulysses subjects him to a terrible torture. The dog of envy, Thersites, who has just called Patroclus Achilles' male whore, slinks along to add a filthy counterpoint and conclude the scene with "Lechery, lechery, still wars and lechery! Nothing else holds fashion" (V.ii.193–194). Nothing could show us more clearly Ulysses' intention to demystify the romantic ideals. The torture of jealousy here is as intense as that in *Othello*. The difference is that the jealousy corresponds to the real deeds of Cressida. We do not find ourselves rooting for the couple and hoping against hope that it will prove to be a misunderstanding. Here we recognize that Troilus is a fool, a noble fool, for believing in Cressida. He is truly alone while the whole meaning of his life is staked on his being with her.

Our sentiments are complex when we contemplate this scene. On the one hand, it is difficult not to pity Troilus and to wish that it would all work out for the best for him. But we are persuaded of Cressida's falseness and know that a man should not live in false trust. Something like this excuses Ulysses' cruelty in sticking Troilus' nose into the mess. He may not be doing it for Troilus' sake, but it is not an unmixed act of cruelty. Othello does not believe in his beloved enough. Troilus believes too much in his. Under his own eyes he sees his beloved give his sleeve to his rival, whereas Othello had to fill in the argument that bridged the gap between his giving Desdemona his handkerchief and its possession by his supposed rival. Each one's heart was attached to the piece of cloth and was ripped out by its misappropriation. Troilus is made to pay a very high price for his opinion that "What's aught but as 'tis valued?" (II.ii.53). The noble soul creates value. But here an overwhelming reality makes it impossible to maintain a love that is not confirmed by its object.

When Troilus has been witness of Diomedes with Cressida, Ulysses says, "All's done, my lord," and Troilus agrees that it is. And Ulysses asks, "Why stay we then?" Troilus is compelled to stay in order to meditate on the meaning of what he has seen with his two eyes. What we witness is an epic culmination of the play's deepest theme, the quarrel between desire and reason. Troilus has always discussed his love as though it were equal or superior to the love of the gods. Belief or faith is his profoundest longing, although for him it is faith in the imaginations that emanate from his eros. He says "credence" gives birth to a hope that is "so obstinately strong" that it "doth invert th'attest of eyes and ears." He concludes on the basis of this logic of the heart with the question, "Was Cressid here?" Ulysses dryly responds that he cannot conjure. Troilus insists he is not mad, but goes on to exhort disbelief of what he has just seen for the sake of "womanhood" (V.ii.114–132). As we have seen, Troilus argues on the premises of moral commonplaces that he cannot bear to call into question. Here the consequence he draws from Cressida's infidelity is the infidelity of all women, especially the infidelity of mothers. The whole family moral order, which depends on the belief in the chastity of women, is collapsing. Of course, Troilus' logic is mad, taking the particular as the same thing as the general. At best, he could say, "Some are, some aren't." But this is a profound reflection of the logic of the heart or love in that when we love, we stake everything on an individual or a particular. If this particular is not the perfection itself of virtue, there is no virtue, and love as we know it disappears. Troilus has already declared himself the enemy of reason and is aware of love's inner necessity. Ulysses coldly accepts the rational conclusions from Cressida's behavior, but refuses to extend its meaning to all women. But Ulysses is emphatically not a lover. There is a war between reason and love. Unequivocal and unqualified love wants to attach a meaning to particular attachment, which reason can never allow.

Troilus piles up questionable premise upon questionable premise and tries to draw a necessary conclusion.

> If beauty have a soul, this is not she;
> If souls guide vows, if vows be sanctimonies,
> If sanctimony be the gods' delight,
> If there be rule in unity itself,
> This is not she. O madness of discourse,
> That cause sets up with and against itself!
> Bifold authority! where reason can revolt
> Without perdition, and loss assume all reason
> Without revolt. This is, and is not, Cressid. (V.ii.137–145)

This is a true conclusion. All of us who are particulars are and are not, partaking of being and nothing at the same time. But love insists on the universality and eternity of its object, and to the extent that its object is another human being, love is therefore either an illusion or a disappointment. True logic leads to human isolation, as one sees in the case of Ulysses himself, who is detached from his rulers and has no visible object of aspiration and no connections of love or friendship. Troilus' rejection of reason is based on a kind of insane attachment to the principle of noncontradiction, which is the very foundation of reason, and to the principle of causality. No speech in Shakespeare states the intellectual premises of love with such clarity. It is truly mad reasoning, but it is reasoning. If men were to turn their gaze to objects that do not admit of contradiction, there would be no problem. The question is whether one can love such objects. Ulysses can contemplate this scene without any need for self-contradiction and accept it with equanimity; he stands for the intransigent application of real reason to all things. But he is hateful to lovers, that is, to most of Shakespeare's audience. I do not think that he wishes to hurt Troilus. There is evidence that he pities him. What Troilus learns causes him to become angry and furious. He cannot learn merely to contemplate, as does Ulysses. The destruction of his ideal makes it impossible for him to live halfway sensibly as he did before. His noble enthusiasm for Cressida, and thus for Helen, and thus for war, has been effectively removed. Ulysses certainly believes that this war is

unreasonable and does what he can to end it. *Troilus and Cressida* is
the only Shakespearean play where reason, understood philosophi-
cally, is the theme.

Next we see the honest and idealistic Trojans prepare for war,
with Priam, Andromache, and Cassandra trying to keep their
men at home while Hector is unshakable in his dedication to honor.
Troilus supports him while chiding him for being too gentle, himself
declaring for all-out war without fair play and without pity. His only
concern now is vengeance, a particular vengeance that he never gets.

The high-mindedness of the Trojans is unrelieved, and off they go
to battle, perfect gentlemen and knights. Hector encounters Achilles,
who has boasted so shamelessly of his superiority to his prey, but who
now gets winded and excuses himself from the fray, alleging that he is
out of shape and will come back when he is in better form. Hector
agrees to this because he lives by the book of chivalry, and how one
wins is more important than winning. Shakespeare presents this in
the style of exposé. "You know the story. Now I will give you the story
behind the story." After a scene where Hector kills a Greek in beautiful armor under which he finds a "Most putrefied core" (V.viii.1),
which is symbolic of what we learn about the Greeks in this play altogether, Hector disarms himself. Achilles appears and then tells his
troop of Myrmidons to surround Hector. When they do, Achilles orders them to kill him. It is, as I have said, a murder, a dastardly deed by
Achilles and the opposite of the kind of death wished for by Hector.
Cressida and Achilles belong together in their trampling on the dignity of love and war. Achilles ties Hector to his horse and drags him
around in ignominious triumph. Achilles is very much what Socrates
says he is in the *Republic*.[14] He beats up on a corpse. But the successful
deed of getting rid of Hector, so long as its nature is not known, guar-
antees Achilles eternal fame. He got a good poet. Troilus screams in
despair at Hector's loss and says that the war is over. In fact, it endured
much longer, but Shakespeare treats it as though it ended here.

Shakespeare's very rough treatment of the spirited, combative
man is, as I have noted, not exclusive to this play. He ridicules Hector's
dressing up of the harsh thing in itself with the formulas of chivalry,
and he more than ridicules the butchery by Achilles. The poetic prejudice in favor of the spirited, heroic man is subjected to a powerful

critique by Shakespeare, just as it is by Plato. Warlike men are necessary, and like most everyone else, I suppose, they have their specific illusions that will enable them to believe in what they are doing. But the world is distorted by illusions, and a wise man must see through them. As far as it is in his power, he tries to mitigate the effect of these illusions. With boyish playfulness Hotspur is really just looking for someone to kill. The much more rational Hal makes fun of Hotspur's dining on deaths. Hal is perfectly willing to kill someone when it is reasonable to do so, and as a matter of fact he kills one notable person, Hotspur. In so doing, he is able to appropriate all of Hotspur's reputation at one stroke. This is reason, or the reasonableness of the political man.[15]

This leads us to a look at Ulysses. He is, I argue, the hero of the play. As we have seen, he does not always appear to be so because he represents something that is not to the taste of the audiences of tragedy or comedy: reason. This play is not satisfying to our moral sense. Achilles is not punished for his evil deeds; neither is Cressida. The only thing that rights the balance is the reasonable and just scheme of Ulysses, who takes the poetry, and hence the dangerous poison of its idealism, out of this war. He accepts it as an ugly business that reflects much of human nature and wishes to return to simple, if not honorable, peace. He is a modest presence in the play; but from his first appearance, he is not only saying the sensible things but manipulating the outcome with his profound sense of the politically necessary and his capacity to know and motivate men's souls. Ulysses does not produce a splendid or even especially just solution, but it is effective so long as wisdom does not become megalomaniacal and believe it can assure just and noble solutions to human problems. Ulysses does not hold that there are just gods upholding a providential order. What is going to be done has to be done by men with all the limitations of men, sometimes masquerading under higher apparent authorities. Ulysses' political scheme conduces, by deeds of questionable justice, to the common good, if one does not treat the common good too grandly. His goal seems to be peace, simple peace, without any need for gilding it, where a man like Ulysses, as shown by his deeds in the *Odyssey,* can take the center of the stage.

What Shakespeare has done in *Troilus and Cressida* is to subject classical heroism to a microscopic analysis. He would seem to underwrite the Christian notion that the Greek virtues are but splendid vices. He does not merely parody love and war, but from a comic perspective shows that it is imaginations and slaughters on which they live. But Shakespeare, unlike the Christian detractors of antiquity, does not join in their criticism of the pride of reason. After the heroes have been put in an acid bath, they all dissolve except for the one man among the Homeric heroes who represents wisdom. In this sense the play is a vindication of the Greeks over the Trojans, and antiquity over modernity. The Greeks have one man who singly counterbalances their ugliness. He is Ulysses *cum* Socrates. As I have said, such a figure is not very suitable to the stage. In Prospero we see a wise man whose gaiety covers over a hardly bearable vision of life. In Ulysses we see the wise man dealing with real life, and it can be a most disheartening experience. The gods and the heroes are unmasked, and the glory that was Greece turns out not to be glory at all. This can appear to be a combination of Enlightenment-style debunking and Célinesque nihilism. But Ulysses really practices neither, for the bleak surroundings serve to set off the beauty and dignity that belong to wisdom alone and to a way of life devoted to truth without illusion. I cannot resist comparing Ulysses to Thucydides, who chronicles without hope the decay of his whole splendid world and gets an austere pleasure from it. It is a solitary life, separated from the common goals and aspirations, one that is too detached for most men to bear. Thucydides represents the theoretical life in its opposition to all the charms of practical life, and so does this isolated Ulysses, who is among the Greeks but not really of them. Shakespeare puts him next to Troilus, the honest and appealing lover, as they together contemplate the spectacle of human vice. Troilus is too involved to enjoy it or accept it. Ulysses is the opposite. There is no question that love and its promises of the unity of two human beings become strongly doubtful from the perspective of reason. What human beings can really share without potential opposition is only reason, and that is pretty thin stuff on which to nourish passionate men and women. Shakespeare's plays about lovers have a kind of irony that does not suit the Romantic temperament. Love is wonderful, but the reasonable observer cannot help seeing through it, at least a bit.

The play ends with a lighthearted address to the audience by Pandarus. In *Troilus and Cressida* very low people, like Patroclus and Thersites, are compared to the poets, and so is Pandarus, who is the only singing poet in the play. He is the pander who makes the connection between poetic imitation and the audience. Somehow a cynical reflection on the bad reputation of poets and actors would seem to follow appropriately from having seen this play. "O traitors and bawds, how earnestly are you set awork, and how ill requited. Why should our endeavour be so loved and the performance so loathed?" (V.x.37–40). Pandarus deals in a tainted kind of love that pleases most people as perhaps does the obscene side of Shakespeare. Pandarus ends by announcing that he and his audience both groan from venereal complaints, bitter accompaniments of the trade of love. In two months he promises his will will be made:

> Till then I'll sweat and seek about for eases,
> And at that time bequeath you my diseases. (V.x.56–57)

These are the last words of the play.

chapter five

THE WINTER'S TALE

The Winter's Tale takes place in Sicily and Bohemia at an uncertain
date, and its characters seem to partake in equal measure of the religion and life of old Greece and Rome and of Christianity. It begins
with the celebration of a classical-style friendship between two kings,
Leontes and Polixenes, who have known each other from childhood
and have a perfect harmony in their reciprocal admiration of each
other's virtues. This very short beginning conveys the joy of confidence and trust combined with the enthusiasm of friendship. Human
association for these two men is natural and a peak of pleasure. They
do not use or need each other, at least not in any narrow sense. They
understand each other, share views, and simply want to be together,
although their kingly responsibilities keep them separate most of the
time.

This glimpse of perfect friendship in action is immediately dis-
turbed by an inexplicable and unmotivated storm of jealousy that destroys the atmosphere of trust and the friendship. Jealousy means
doubt about the sexual fidelity of one to whom a person is attached.[1]
Leontes suddenly comes to believe that his friend and his wife have
had illicit relations. Leontes is both friend and husband, but there has
never before been any tension between the two kinds of attachment.
His wife, Hermione, seems to be just like him and to have adopted his
friend as her friend. The openness and lack of reserve characteristic of
friendship are not usual between a married woman and a man not her

All parenthetical citations in this chapter are to Shakespeare's *The Winter's Tale*, ed. J. H. P. Pafford,
Arden Edition (1963; rpt. London: Routledge, 1988).

husband. But their friendship is apparently part of the old friendship between her husband and his friend. The sudden explosion of angry jealousy brings to light a problem about a married woman's blameless friendship with a man. The suspicions aroused make it impossible to have that confidence required for men and women to be together without tincture of erotic involvement. Moreover their new condition of marriage also raises doubts about the possibility of friendship between married men.

The arousal of jealousy, which is so sudden and seems such a mystery, needs interpretation. Leontes' jealousy is unlike that experienced by Troilus, whose beloved is guilty, and is akin to that of Othello, whose beloved is not guilty. Leontes' case, however, is much more extreme than that of Othello, who must be seduced into his passion by a subtle devil. Leontes' whole vision of the world changes in an instant and without provocation. Shakespeare usually treats this kind of terrible passion as a mistake on the part of the man. *Cymbeline* gives us another such case. What is so unusual about Leontes in this play is the speed of his change from trust to certitude of disloyalty. As soon as this takes place, the old world of friendship disappears. There is reconciliation and a happy ending, but it does not restore the old world, and it gives a definite primacy to marriage over friendship. Shakespeare seems preoccupied with the distrust in men about the genuineness of women's attachment and what it leads to. Shakespeare is fully aware of the difficulty of real unity between human beings, even, or especially, in love matters. But it is indicative of his temper that he concentrates so much on the unfoundedness of such suspicion, and hence affirms the possibility of unconstrained connectedness.

This inexplicable transformation is almost miraculous since one cannot treat Leontes as a sickly, weak soul, prone to suspicions. In Shakespeare one can almost always get guidance as to the character of a man by the kind of friends he has and how they behave with him. Not only is Leontes' wife a most remarkable woman, with whom he seems to have had up to now a free and open relationship, unstained by doubts, but he has also evidently been faithful and irreproachable in friendship. There are no villains in Leontes' entourage. On the contrary, they are all honest and forthright persons who serve loyally because of the character of the man they serve and are used to speaking with him on a level of frank equality. He has no flatterers, which makes it all the more difficult for him to follow the logic of his jealousy, because no one supports him in it. I can clarify the problem of his jealousy only by what immediately precedes it (I.ii.1–108). Leontes has failed to persuade Polixenes to prolong his stay with them in Sicily. He turns the task of persuasion over to Hermione, who succeeds. After she has done so, she starts asking questions about what the two friends were like when they were young. Polixenes tells her of their perfect joy in each other's company, which was most characterized by innocence. Polixenes makes it clear that he means by innocence sexual innocence and refers, pagan though he is, to the doctrine of original sin. Prior to sexual development they could have answered to heaven, except for the guilt associated with that sin that all men inherit, the Fall. Hermione slyly picks up on this and suggests that he, and perhaps her husband too, have "tripp'd since" that time of innocence. Polixenes rather ambiguously replies that there have been temptations since "the stronger blood" was born in them. She playfully returns to the assault and says that Polixenes' wife and she will answer for any sins connected with them. She refers to their married sexual relations here as sins, but affirms that there will be no punishment for them if there were no other sins committed with others. The formulation of her statement ("that you slipp'd not / With any but with us") could be interpreted to mean that it would be all right for Polixenes to have had sexual relations with her, although this is clearly not her intention. But she is playing around with an erotic theme, the difficulty of taming men's desires. It is not certain that Leontes hears these remarks. He has evidently been walking at some distance in order to allow his wife to persuade Polixenes to stay. He enters the conversation again at the end of this colloquy. When Hermione tells him that Polixenes will stay, he responds that she has never spoken to better purpose. She then plays a coquettish game with him, asking, "Never?" She talks about the nature of women and how they may be ridden more effectively with soft kisses than with spurs. She insists that he repeat what she said at the end of his long and hard courtship, "I am yours for ever." She thus links her persuasion of Polixenes to her giving herself to Leontes. Her first good speech "earn'd a royal husband," the second, a friend. With that, she grasps Polixenes' hand.

And then it happens. Suddenly Leontes lives in a world of temptations and betrayals. Every deed and gesture has an explicit sexual meaning. Lust is everywhere, and it cannot be controlled by the rules of morality. The doubts about sexual attraction, which are always le-

gitimate because thought and the movements of the sexual organs are
not simply subject to will, become certitudes, and the whole world
must be corrected. The first thoughts are about the legitimacy of one's
children, then the ridicule attracted by a cuckold, a ridicule earned by
the prejudice that a real man must be attractive to his wife always and
exclusive of all others. Then there are thoughts of revenge, dignified
as claims of simple justice. There is the fear that the whole world gives
witness to the adultery, but there is also the certainty that those who do
not see what he sees must be guilty of blindness and faithlessness.
Everything is in the belief of the king, and all the subjects must support the king's belief or be subjected to the most terrible punishments.
What we see is sexual doubt turning gentle and legitimate kingship
into a tyranny that resembles the demands of a jealous god, rather than
those of natural human attachment. As is always the case with love
suspected of betrayal, the principle of noncontradiction is called into
question. The belief that something can come from nothing seems to
be required. Othello suffers this delusion, as does Troilus. Nothing
else can account for such transformations from virtue to sin. Reason
no longer rules the world; tyranny is the only way to forestall chaos.
There is no solid center, opposites "co-act," and saint and sinner
emerge from the same source. These are the mad affections of the man
whose life is founded upon the necessity of another person's being always attracted to him.

The jealousy of Leontes follows its course. He orders his minister
Camillo to poison Polixenes. Camillo suffers the conflict of the man
who owes loyalty to a tyrant and is commanded to do something immoral. He leaves Leontes to follow Polixenes. When Leontes' tyrannical passion is deprived of the satisfaction of killing Polixenes, it
turns on Hermione, whom he imprisons, and then on the daughter
born to Hermione in prison, whom he orders to be abandoned to the
elements in a remote spot outside his kingdom. He stages an inquisi-
tion accusing Hermione not only of adultery, but of conspiracy with
Polixenes and Camillo to overthrow him. She has only her own testimony to defend herself against unfeeling and unhearing tyranny. Her
sole supporter is the fierce Paulina, who will be her apostle and aveng-
ing spirit. Suspicions and unknowable intentions are more important
than any deeds. A premise that all human beings, and especially
women, are hot and unreliable has been established. This awareness
makes trust impossible for those who care. Trials and prisons are the

only remedy. Sexual desire, like heresy, an unknowable disposition of the mind, becomes the central object of justice.

When, in the midst of Hermione's trial, Leontes' ambassadors interrupt the proceedings to announce that the Delphic oracle proclaims her chaste and everyone else innocent, he simply dismisses the news. He has a new source of certitude that replaces his belief in the Delphic god. Immediately he is punished by the announcement of the death of his young prince, Mamillius, the only one of whom he is sure. Hermione faints. The death of the innocent boy causes the extinction of the tyrant's jealousy as quickly as it came into being. But it is too late. Hermione also dies, and the baby daughter, abandoned at his command, is lost. Now the atmosphere of Sicily is guilt and repentance, and Paulina becomes the minister of a cult devoted to the dead queen and her son. Leontes' tears at their chapel will be his recreation and his exercise.

Antigonus, charged by Leontes to get rid of the baby, deposited her on the Bohemian coast, and was himself immediately eaten by a bear. But here in Bohemia in a rustic setting that defies time and the distinctions between ancients and moderns, Shakespeare prepares the healing of the Sicilian wounds with the salubrious aid of nature. The characters here are beyond or beneath the changes of regimes and religions, and the necessary customs of the courts that differentiate them. We have a shepherd and his clownish son and a singing thief who has the same name and habits as Odysseus' grandfather.[2] Here, innocence and the spirit of comedy provide the seedbed for an overcoming of the tragic darkness of both the Sicilian and the Bohemian courts.

Act IV is devoted almost exclusively to this pastoral dream of reconciliation with nature, and here eroticism frolics untainted by its fearful doppelgänger, jealousy. Time, as a chorus, introduces Act IV in a play where the distinctiveness of various times in human history is treated so cavalierly by Shakespeare. This provides a helpful guide to Shakespeare's understanding of that terrible master to which our lives are subject.

> since it is in my power
> To o'erthrow law, and in one self-born hour

To plant and o'erwhelm custom. Let me pass
The same I am, ere ancient'st order was,
Or what is now receiv'd. I witness to
The times that brought them in; so shall I do
To th' freshest things now reigning, and make stale
The glistering of this present, as my tale
Now seems to it. (IV.i.7–15)

This is exactly the opposite of the way our contemporaries would think of time, which seems to be a co-conspirator with our necessary subordination to our own time. Time, as it expresses itself here, permits the playwright to see the coming into being and passing away of laws and customs, and hence to liberate himself from and laugh at them. Those laws and customs are not consubstantial with time. The spirit of this play is not to take the present, in particular here the new order of things in Sicily, seriously or to be overwhelmed by becoming and decay, but to look for a permanent standard and satisfactions outside the ephemeral systems of belief. Plays are subject to the immediate tastes of the audience, but, as Shakespeare indicates, the true playwright can teach an audience to despise the current attractions. Shakespeare, in such works as *Troilus and Cressida*, *Cymbeline*, and *The Winter's Tale*, plays very fast and loose with what we would call history, although as we have seen in *Romeo and Juliet* and *Antony and Cleopatra*, he can also stay very close to the real spirit of a particular time and place. *The Winter's Tale* and *Cymbeline* are among Shakespeare's very last plays, and here he permits himself the wildest flights of his kind of historical imagination. The very last play, *The Tempest*, is altogether the opposite, in that it maintains the classical unities of time and place, perhaps more rigorously than any other Shakespearean play. But this exception would only confirm the late freedom of Shakespeare from constraints normally imposed on us by the age in which we live, because in *The Tempest* we have only a dream, literally a play, which is outside of any historical situation, although it is related to one, Renaissance Italy. All three of these plays allow Shakespeare to show forth his ripest wisdom, looking at the laws and regimes of nations and the coming into being and passing away of religions from a perspective beyond history. Time, for Shakespeare, contrary to our belief, is not the destroyer of nature as a standard, but nature's accomplice in revealing what is always as opposed to what is merely made by man.

This discourse of Time about time is the introduction to the great celebration of nature.

Act IV, scene iv, is one of the longest in Shakespeare, almost 850 lines. In it we find a pastoral romance complicated by reflections on nature and convention. A prince loves a shepherdess, and there are two plots to use the pair of lovers, Camillo's to get back to Sicily, and Autolycus' to better himself ("all the world loves a lover," because lovers are so easy to use). The central theme throughout is the innocent, passionate, and restorative love between Florizel, the son of Polixenes, and the shepherdess Perdita, the lost daughter of Leontes, now grown up. This affair belongs with those of Romeo and Juliet and of Ferdinand and Miranda as an example of simple, uncomplicated love at first sight without the slightest admixture of vanity on either side, a mutual attraction of beautiful youngsters lucky enough to have found each other before less happy experiences have made them distinguish between body and soul in erotic matters. With them there is an eternity in the present, a forgetfulness of what time will do to them as well as to nations and their laws. Romeo and Juliet in the setting of Renaissance Christian Verona almost necessarily end in tragedy. Ferdinand and Miranda have an untroubled courtship and prospects for an untroubled future under the guidance of Prospero. Their marriage will result in the union of two realms, Milan and Naples. Florizel and Perdita are helped by nature, by the former's intense self-control, fortune, and a bit of wisdom contributed by Camillo. For them it all works out, but their success is less realistic than Romeo and Juliet's failure; the atmosphere of a fiction is maintained throughout. As in *The Tempest*, all petty motives are banished by the intensity of the love of the beautiful shared by the two partners.

The cloud on Florizel and Perdita's horizon is formed by the conflict between the conventional inequality of the two and the authority of Florizel's father to enforce that inequality. The greatest loves are founded on inclination that is free of the constraints of propriety and duty. The beauties of the body obviously leap over all artificial fences. The prejudice of fathers is that breeding determines the soul and cannot be properly judged by youngsters whose bodily passions lead them. Of course the fathers, especially when kings, are really less interested in the satisfactions of their children's love than in the succession to their kingdoms. This is a point Rousseau makes, unequivocally taking the side of the children, if they are properly educated.[3] Shakespeare, who is usually respectful of the conventions, vigorously sides here with Florizel. But the father undeniably has a point. Ordinarily a boy who meets a country lass and becomes infatuated requires some restraint in order to be sure that he has found a suitable mate. In one of those twists that allow Shakespeare to preserve the conventional moral order, the object of Florizel's passion is really a princess. The issue is not noble versus commoner, but how to recognize a princess. Florizel appears to have that instinct. Shakespeare, who knew himself to be a commoner and also knew himself superior to all the nobles and the kings, does not permit the awareness of his own situation to determine the orders possible for society. He admirably mixes nature and convention; in doing this he finds a place in the world for his uncommon commonness.

This mixing is discussed by Polixenes and Perdita in the scene where she distributes flowers (IV.iv.70–167). Polixenes and Camillo, disguised as very old men, receive what they call winter flowers and would prefer to have a little less explicit reminder of their mortality. Perdita says there are flowers that would be appropriate but they are nature's bastards (which is what her own father suspected her to be as Polixenes' child), and she will have none of them. She wants nothing of an art that "shares with great creating nature." For her, nature alone produces legitimate offspring; art produces bastards. Her view is the opposite of that of kings. She has a kind of religion of nature, untouched and unassisted by human doings. Her very person makes a great case for her faith. Polixenes, accepting her view that nature should be supreme, argues that though there are indeed arts that are not natural, they are guided by a hierarchy that nature itself makes. He stands for the naturalness of the higher powers of intellect that intervene in raw nature for the sake of preserving the "intention" of nature. Polixenes makes a point opposite to that made by Melville in *The Confidence Man*, where a character asserts his eyes were made not by nature but by an oculist in Philadelphia.[4] The oculist has an art of which there is no natural pattern, but it is on the basis of study of the natural perfection of the eyes that the oculist can correct this particular case of weakness of sight. Thus the eyes are enabled to fulfill their universal vocation, a vocation not made by the oculist. Such a study or art of natural perfection generally would be philosophy, which judges where the specialized arts fulfill nature and where they contravene it. This is the most delicate of arts and the one least easily recognizable in those who possess it. But it is a much truer relation to nature than the acceptance of whatever raw nature produces as deserving of reverence. Perdita is the unconscious innocent who will have to be guided in her social relations by persons wiser than herself. Shakespeare's own art, which is one of the profoundest themes of this play, is close to the ones propounded by Polixenes, and admits of the necessity of art for understanding and living in the nature so dear to Perdita.

Polixenes, against his will, is somewhat taken by this charming girl. His reflections on art by no means make him a philosopher. But he is a ruler, and rulers exercise a kind of prudence in the government of a state and its people that is akin to the universal governance of reason in the world, a point made by the gardeners in *Richard II,* who use their rational governance of their garden as a standard to criticize Richard's governance of the state.[5] Unfortunately, the kingly art is most usually perverted and does not look to human nature and its fulfillment in making its decisions. Only Plato's *Republic* attempts to bring together the art of the natural whole and the art of the city in making philosophers kings. Polixenes, under the influence of this girl, makes the following reflection:

> You see, sweet maid we marry
> A gentler scion to the wildest stock,
> And make conceive a bark of baser kind
> By bud of nobler race. (IV.iv.92–95)

Here he speaks as the kind of eugenicist recommended in *The Republic,* where the philosopher kings are really marriage experts, mixing the stocks or natures of men to produce healthy citizens. Polixenes does not appear to recognize that he is producing plausible grounds for the marriage of his son to a wild child. For a moment his natural vision overcomes his political one.

Shakespeare gives the sympathies of the audience entirely to rebellious Florizel, not to his kingly father, Polixenes. Florizel maintains the outward forms of respect, but he is absolutely intransigent in his disobedience. Love is his only guide, his polar star. Perhaps Shakespeare so unambiguously takes sides because this couple is a kind of announcement of a new order that will take the place of a gloomy and neurotic old one, where regrets and guilts reign. In *The Tempest* we are entirely on the side of Prospero when he brutalizes Ferdinand, but this is because we are persuaded Prospero is wise and will bring things to the best end. Polixenes, on the other hand, is overtaken by a sudden rage that threatens death. After the dance of the satyrs, Polixenes unmasks himself and there is a risk that the mayhem that took place in Sicily sixteen years before will be repeated here, strangely turning on the parentage of this same child. This is not the sexual jealousy of Leontes, but it is again a tyranny attempting to control natural inclination. Florizel immediately plans flight with his beloved, and in this he contrasts sharply with Romeo, who first despairs and then relies on the superartificial schemes of his priestly accomplice. Florizel then accepts sensible counsel from Camillo, and instead of giving himself to the fortunes of the sea heads to Sicily. While he himself is deceiving Florizel in order to prepare his return home, Camillo suggests that Florizel deceive Leontes. The advice turns out to be good, but that is partly due to chance; and the interestedness of Camillo is food for thought about the counselors to princes.

The center of this scene is given to Autolycus with his high spirits and thief's intentions. At scene's end he is an instrument of the recognition, an instrumentality in which he sees possible advancement. Contrary to instinct he helps Florizel but unluckily gets no credit for it. He appears in the scene first as a purveyor of all those trinkets for female adornment that are so repulsive to Perdita. Florizel concurs that none of these vanities will mean anything to his Perdita. But Autolycus nevertheless makes a great hit with the other girls and reveals a permanent aspect of the nature of most women. He also sells ballads and sings them with the girls. The ballads are obscene, and Perdita, who is like Juliet unabashedly sensual, assures her brother, the Clown, that she does not care to think of such things. But the ballads are great entertainments and give the news of the day. In Act V the miraculous doings at the court of Sicily are said to be the stuff out of which ballads are made, although surpassing the art of ballad makers (V.ii.23–25). To put it bluntly, Autolycus is one of those figures invented by Shakespeare to represent at least a part of himself. He is an utter rogue, with nothing but contempt for the law. He never lets thoughts of his fate in the afterlife poison his pleasures of the day. He steals the money of his spiritual inferiors but reflects,

> How blessed are we that are not simple men!
> Yet nature might have made me as these are;
> Therefore I will not disdain. (IV.iv.746–748)

The simple are not blessed, but they are human and deserve human kindness. A man like Autolycus cannot help taking advantage of them, but he recognizes that it is nature, not himself, who deserves the credit for his superiority. He does not, however, concur with those, in particular Rousseau and Kant, who made the same observation and drew the consequence that nature contributes no part to human worth or dignity. No writer of entertainments for the people can avoid the recognition that a large part of the audience is made up of the simple who love vulgar displays and will always have a taste for untruth.

Autolycus is a supramoral character for whom Shakespeare wickedly gives us some sympathy. He does little harm, only engaging in petty thefts of property, and provides us with a liberating laughter in harmony with the lovely, but perhaps only momentary, rediscovery of natural paradise. When he fails to get recognition and promotion at the court, he sweetly recognizes his kind could never belong there. This is Shakespeare's comment on the question, raised earlier, about the place of his own commonness in the hierarchy of the court and the nobility. He wins out over them because they become his characters. Autolycus engages in a charming bit of casuistry to prove that his loyalty to Florizel is not in contradiction to his profession, because not informing the king of his son's plans is to defy the authority of a king (IV.iv.832–843). Thus we get a certain kind of explanation of Shakespeare's knavery, which supports the true moral order. In this late play Shakespeare permits himself the pleasure of putting the poet on stage. He is ridiculous, beneath the level of the great deeds acted on the stage, and does not in any way further the plot. He has only a fugitive place in the world of action, but he casts a revealing light on the actions. As the First Gentleman says, when telling of the miraculous events that have taken place, "The dignity of this act was worth the audience of kings and princes; for by such was it acted" (V.ii.79–80). The line between performing an act and acting (in the theatrical sense) is blurred. The illusion of the theater is that the deeds it mimics are the most important thing. But Shakespeare may very well think that "the play's the thing," that his stories present the highest thing, the moment of understanding, telling the story for all posterity. Autolycus is lighthearted toward the things that men and women take most seriously but which are not so serious from the point of view of the poet or that of knowledge.

In Act V, scene i, we first get a picture of the gloomy world of Sicily with its guilt-ridden king living only to blame himself and for the sake of repentance. This world is orchestrated by Paulina, the apostle of the martyred Hermione, who spends her time reminding him of the perfection he has lost and of the fact that he *killed* her. She puts herself in charge of Leontes' private life and makes him promise that he will not marry without her permission, even though there are the most pressing political reasons for him to marry again. The contrast between the this-worldly, one may say classical period of Leontes' rule and this one could hardly be more complete. Paulina preaches indifference to the succession, a problem that is absolutely central in Shakespeare's view of monarchy, as we learn from the history plays. Paulina of course knows Hermione is alive; but at this stage we do not know it, and we see only the terrible setting of personal guilt and political negligence promoted by her. And we must remember that Paulina has kept this going for sixteen years (IV.i.6). Without the discovery of Perdita, who knows how long she would have persevered? Certainly Leontes deserves punishment, but in fact neither Hermione nor Perdita is dead. The only dead one is the little boy, Mamillius, and the one really shocking aspect of the play is that he is nearly forgotten. He is remembered only by Leontes, and does not seem to play a role in Paulina's plan, for he would have stood in the way of Perdita's succession to the throne. She is the disciple and promoter of a cult devoted almost exclusively to Hermione.

When the arrival and great beauty of Perdita are reported by a most unusual servant, Paulina invokes the sacred name, "O Hermione," and says that the servant is forgetting his own writing, which asserted that Hermione "was not to be equall'd" (V.i.95–101). In both *Cymbeline* and *The Winter's Tale,* plays where sudden jealousy perverts trusting love, persons on the stage are said to be writers who teach something. There is a scripture that accompanies jealousy. In *Cymbeline* Posthumus Leonatus (note the similarity of names), after the most vivid of all the expressions of jealous imaginations—

> Perchance he spoke not, but
> Like a full-acorn'd boar, a German one,
> Cried "O!" and mounted;—

says, "I'll write against them, / Detest them, curse them."[6] The writings are an important part of the education of the adherents to the faith. The writings about Hermione are not necessarily in contradiction with the writings of Posthumus Leonatus against women. A new kind of woman characterized above all by chastity or purity becomes the center of this religion.

Although we are irresistibly inclined to believe that Hermione is not guilty, one ought to remember that, unlike Desdemona and Imogen, Hermione is not proved on the stage to be free of a guilty relation with Polixenes, and that Polixenes, in scene iii, calls himself the cause of Leontes' sufferings (one way or another, out of this affair Polixenes' offspring will reign in Sicily). The issue for Paulina here is not the proof of Hermione's innocence but the establishment of her as beyond criticism, whether or not she bore a child by a great king who was not her husband. Mamillius resembled his father, and in this Hermione was like the mare named Justice, as told by Aristotle, whose foals always resembled the stallions who engendered them.[7] Perdita resembles Hermione. The role of the father is reduced. The scriptor-servant engages in an exchange with Paulina in response to her reproach, admitting that the faith is likely to be forgotten under the influence of the present unless there is someone there to remind him.

SERVANT: Pardon, madam:
> The one I have almost forgot,—your pardon,—
> The other, when she has obtain'd your eye,
> Will have your tongue too. This is a creature,
> Would she begin a sect, might quench the zeal
> Of all professors else; make proselytes
> Of who she but bid follow.
PAULINA: How! not women?

SERVANT: Women will love her, that she is a woman
   More worth than any man; men, that she is
   The rarest of all women. (V.i.103–112)

This kind of religious language and appropriate accompanying feeling dominate the whole of Act V. This new religion overcomes the jealousy of women toward other women because this chosen woman is
proved to be superior to man, showing how women can use the combination of attraction and guilt to accomplish the destruction of the old
male-dominated world.

   Leontes' meeting with Florizel and Perdita provides a mixture of
pleasure and remorse. He is pleased by these unabashed lovers and
pleased thus by proxy to regain contact with his old friend Polixenes.
But it also reminds him again of all that has happened. He says that
he lost a couple, meaning presumably Perdita and Mamillius, who
"might thus have stood" as does the "gracious couple" standing before him. Leontes gives evidence of a certain confusion since his
"couple" would have been brother and sister and would not properly
have been "thus." He wishes that their stay be a good one because
Florizel has a "holy father," against whose sacred person he has committed a sin. He interprets his lack of issue as heaven's punishment for
that sin (V.i.123–137, 167–177). He filters the natural consequences
of his jealousy through the gods, who continue to punish him and provide cosmic guilt for him.

   Polixenes will arrive soon, angry at his son for his defection, at
Perdita, and at all those who may have conspired with them. His anger
is also death-threatening. Florizel asserts that fortune can stand in the
way of his marriage to Perdita, but that it cannot alter his love, which
appears to be the one absolute beyond fortune. He gives Leontes the
occasion to be the one who softens his father. He tells Leontes that to
him his "father will grant precious things as trifles." Leontes, unable to
stop himself, says that then he will beg Florizel's precious mistress
for himself (V.i.223–225). The old king is erotically aroused by her.
He does not know that she is his daughter. Shakespeare's erotic imagination, which we have seen to be so active in *Measure for Measure*,
tests the relation between natural attraction and the sacred laws. He
does this in a way that is not shocking to his audience, although
perhaps it should be. There is a similar scene in *Cymbeline* when
Guiderius and Arviragus, living as children of nature but heirs to the

throne, are sexually attracted to a boy who is actually their sister.[8] That scene poses a special problem because if you clean it up on one side it becomes all the dirtier on the other. There is more plasticity in sexual desire than conventional propriety admits. This scene in *The Winter's Tale* is a gentle and ironic presentation of the perpetual Oedipus question. The ever watchful Paulina reminds Leontes, not that sexual desire is improper, but that the lost Hermione is so much more attractive, even though she is not to be enjoyed in this world. Leontes excuses himself by saying that he saw Hermione in Perdita. Of course many fathers could say such things of their daughters. In fatherly fashion Leontes agrees to help the young lovers if they are truly chaste.

The classic recognition scene is not presented on the stage but is told by onlookers. This happy ending is farcically implausible, but it does the job in alleviating situations of revenge and remorse. The two old friends are reconciled. There is a survivor of Leontes' wrath. She is given a worth for Polixenes in addition to her beauty that makes her an acceptable bride, and love is given its due. This love will be the grounds for a new beginning, although one that comprehends the historical facts that preceded it. The scene ends with Autolycus' last appearance in the company of the newly ennobled shepherd and his son, the Clown. This scene is slapstick, for these are absurd gentlemen, but it shows Autolycus' capacity to adjust to a world in which the simple, the shepherds and the clowns, inherit the earth. He flatters them with all his habitual irony, and they agree to protect him. Autolycus will make do in whatever dispensation happens to dominate (V.ii.124–175).

Act V, scene iii, the culmination of *The Winter's Tale*, is one of the strangest tales in all of literature. We learned in scene ii that there was a statue of Hermione in the keeping of Paulina made by the Italian master Julio Romano. This egregious anachronism has shocked centuries' worth of critics, but it points to the meaning of the play. The praise of the artist is extravagant and is another important reflection on the meaning of art and manifestation of Shakespeare's unusual self-consciousness about it. He, Julio Romano, is good enough to steal nature's customers from her, but there are two immediate qualifications to his superiority over nature. First, he is only nature's perfect ape. His superiority might consist in producing beauty that nature intends but never actually produces. Something like this is suggested by Paulina, who refers to Hermione, the subject of the statue in question.

> If, one by one, you wedded all the world,
> Or from the all that are took something good,
> To make a perfect woman, she you kill'd
> Would be unparallel'd. (V.i.13–16)

The second defect, however, is decisive: he does not himself have eternity, which, according at least to the Gentleman who says all this, is solely in the possession of nature and makes it the supreme authority of all. And he cannot put breath in his work. The statue is a long-lived reminder of unattainable perfection, and at the same time a great consolation for those who have lost and longed for Hermione. The entire company goes to see this statue, "in hope of answer." The pilgrimage to the statue is set in motion by Perdita's hearing the tale of her mother's death.

> she did, with an "Alas," I would fain say, bleed tears, for I am
> sure my heart wept blood. Who was most marble, there changed
> colour; some swooned, all sorrowed: if all the world could have
> seen't, the woe had been universal. (V.ii.87–91)

Here we see marble turn into flesh, which parallels the role of the statue. Natural limits are surpassed under the influence of love and sorrow. This kind of statue and the tearful worship of it were and are well known in the Roman Catholic church, where sinning men and women have felt consolation and even response from statues, in a worship that has brought down on that Church the reproach of idolatry. Such statues have long existed, but this one had to be done by a Renaissance artist.

Paulina is the great animator. She has kept Hermione in her house for sixteen years. Leontes says that he has never seen the statue of Hermione when he visited Paulina's gallery. Paulina is apparently an art lover and has her own gallery like those of Renaissance princes and prelates. Since Hermione's statue is the greatest thing that an artist has ever made, she kept it separate, and she calls that spot not a gallery but a chapel. Paulina milks Leontes' first sight of the statue for all the regrets and sorrows imaginable. But Leontes, presumably under the influence of having seen Perdita, notices that there are more wrinkles on the statue of Hermione than when he knew her. This is not too good a harbinger of the erotic attractiveness of the statue were it to come to life. But Polixenes enthusiastically chimes in that the wrinkles do not exceed the original by much. Leontes returns to his worshipful attitude; and Perdita, first insisting in a traditional Catholic excuse that she is not superstitious, kneels and implores the statue's blessing, beginning her address with the word "Lady." This is all quite clearly an artistic aping, not of nature, but of the cult of Mary. Paulina then prepares them for more "amazement," which, if they are not ready to receive, they should leave the chapel immediately. She is about to exercise "magic" and professes fear that she will be thought to be a witch, "assisted / By wicked powers." She announces that "It is requir'd / You do awake your faith." She is mistress of ceremonies to a miracle. Hermione comes to life and the whole scene ends in present satisfaction. However, the disposition toward Hermione and her suffering, so carefully nourished by Paulina, will remain (V.iii.44–155).

Hermione was an unusually attractive, frank, intelligent, and open woman. But her experience of the vulnerability of relations on this earth, the suspicions and distrust of men, and the tragic loss of her children, give her finally a delicacy and depth that are conveyed to us by the description of her statue and her one speech after her resurrection expressing her love of her daughter. There are two other great women in Shakespeare who are victims of male jealousy, Desdemona and Imogen, and who as a result of the suffering imposed upon them by it and in response to the ugly, sinful description of sexual desire, become something more than they were and something new in the world. Desdemona is the pure victim in the tragedy; the other two, in what are called the Romances, plays that defy the classic categories of the drama, are spared by Shakespeare and become the gentle civilizers of the men, who perpetually expiate a crime of distrust of their relatedness to their women, and are refined by the self-consciously guilty love of them. Hermione's tears are imitations of Mater Dolorosa's, and her smiles through her tears are reconciliations and redemptions.

Shakespeare seems to have thought that Christianity effected a deepening of women and a new sensitivity of men to them. The manliness of men was diminished by this series of experiences, but the femininity of women and their power over men were greatly enhanced. The great pre-Christian portraits of women, Coriolanus' mother, Volumnia, Brutus' wife, Portia, and Cleopatra, are in their own ways extremely impressive. But there is among them none so deeply human as Desdemona or Hermione, or even Juliet. The cult of women in the tradition of chivalry, which is ridiculed in *Troilus and Cressida*, does, when shorn of its mumbo jumbo and histrionic, superhuman character, give women an influence that permeates all of life, from the quest for glory to the attachment to children, an influence absent in the ancient world. The souls of women have become more interesting than they ever were, and Shakespeare is the poet of women at least as much as he is of men. He clearly represents much madness, and many wounds to the souls of men and women, brought about by the coming of Christianity to the world, but he also chronicles great gains made in this history. It is not clear that he believes that there was a transformation or progress in wisdom beyond the kind one finds in Ulysses. But the possibilities of the human soul revealed by the new dispensation are worthy of contemplation by the philosophers and of imitation by the poets. In this play, where Shakespeare frees himself from the constraints of time in order to show us the things to which it gave birth, he puts on the stage a classical simplicity, the arrival of the Old Testament's jealousy, Christianity's turn to otherworldly hopes, loves and guilts, and something new that is all his own.

Jealousy seems to be the critical change, bringing new doubts and new forms of scrutiny. Modern Italy, as opposed to the ancient Rome that it replaced, seems to play a critical role in the transmission of this passion. It is the diabolical Iago who makes Othello jealous just for the sake of doing so, and Iachimo who makes Posthumus Leonatus jealous for the sake of proving a point. In *Cymbeline*, the dramatic date of which is the closest in Shakespeare's plays to the birth of Jesus,[9] Posthumus Leonatus goes to Rome to meet what is obviously a modern Italian villain and returns to a Britain on the brink of being Romanized and, in the long run, Christianized. These two plays, *Cymbeline* and *The Winter's Tale*, are the poet's phenomenology of the spirit.

The something new I just mentioned is Shakespeare himself and gets its expression in the play in Julio Romano, the artist who supposedly re-creates Hermione, the new Hermione with her new position bestowed on her for her sufferings. Julio Romano was a Renaissance artist, and so is Shakespeare. Romano was also an Italian, and Shakespeare is indebted to Italy for many things, not only the Catholic Christianity that one finds there, but also the corrupt but liberating political teachings of Machiavelli along with his religious criticism, and the notion of a special vocation of art. The Renaissance meant, if it meant anything, the rebirth of classical antiquity under the aspect of beauty. It was a rebirth or new life of art, emancipated from its subordination to religion. The experience of all those great artists was the rediscovery of beauty, beauty of bodies, living, breathing, desiring bodies, not bodies seen under the aspect of original sin or diminished by unrepresentable expectations of another life and world. They cast off world-weariness and felt themselves again in the prime of mankind's youth. The beauty of bodies, certainly problematic but also seen as divinatory, again became at least the beginning point. These painters would, on the one hand, turn again to the discredited heroes of antiquity and their deeds in war and in love, but, on the other hand, still devote themselves to the stories of the Christians and especially to that of the Virgin Mother and her Child, painted and sculpted, however, in a way that recalled classical sensuality and love of the body. They effected a kind of reconciliation between divine aspirations and the senses. This was to usher in an era of delight and a rebirth of both politics and love.

chapter six

HAL AND FALSTAFF

As a farewell to Shakespeare, we will look at one of the most unusual and powerful connections in his universe. Prince Hal, the future Henry V and, according to Shakespeare, perhaps the greatest of all English kings, has an intense involvement with Falstaff, a very surprising sort of associate for a man who has such a high vocation. Hal becomes a ruler equipped with all the political virtues: he succeeds, at least in his own lifetime, in bringing an end to the plague of civil war, establishing his own monarchy solidly, and expanding England's territory and influence. He has none of the defects of the other kings Shakespeare treats. His rule provides a textbook for future rulers, which could find its place among Plutarch's *Lives of Illustrious Men* and also satisfy Machiavelli's stern rules for the guidance of a prince. He was the son of a serious and highly moral king, but he chose to spend his youth with a fat, old, lecherous thief. Shakespeare, in the two *Henry IV* plays, which are presumably dedicated to the serious business of reestablishing the authority of the kings in England, spends an extraordinary amount of time putting the frivolous and immoral adventures of Hal and Falstaff on the stage. This is very curious, and his reasons are not quite evident. The story is not simply that of a young man who fools around while waiting to assume the throne. Hal from early on is too calculating and cold a man simply to idle, and we can, I believe, assume that his involvement with Falstaff reveals a part

All parenthetical citations in this chapter are to Shakespeare's *King Henry IV, Part I*, ed. A. R. Humphreys, Arden Edition (1960; rpt. London: Routledge, 1988) or *Part II*, ed. A. R. Humphreys, Arden Edition (1966; rpt. London: Routledge, 1988).

of his taste, which is visible only prior to his becoming king, but remains a hidden aspect of his character when he does rule. In some sense one might say that in *Henry IV, Parts I and II* one sees a kind of education of Hal, not entirely unlike the education of another world-historical rascal, the *Education of Cyrus* invented by Machiavelli's rival Xenophon.[1]

And this relationship is really *invented* by Shakespeare inasmuch as Falstaff is an almost total fabrication, an exception in the history plays, which are in general fairly faithful to the historical record. Somehow Shakespeare had to have this antic fellow, who is not part of history, present in history in order to make his point. He is an Enobarbus in spades. He is also not unlike Autolycus, another Shakespearean invention—a minion of the moon, i.e., a thief and a balladeer. Falstaff is willing to have sex with man, woman, or child (Part II, II.i.14–17), is riddled with venereal diseases, always drunk, a colossal glutton, and moreover, a blasphemer, a superior rhetorician, a man of great wit, and an exemplar of a kind of rationalism. For all of his vices he is one of Shakespeare's most engaging characters. He tramples on all of the rules, divine and human, without becoming repulsive to us. Shakespeare works this wonder by keeping Falstaff's thefts within relatively benign limits and showing that in spite of his bombast, he does not do bodily harm to people. His two loose women, Mistress Quickly and Doll Tearsheet, quarrel with him but love him. He is not actively leading conspiracies, nor is he a traitor to his friends. In general he is the beloved king of the Boar's Head Tavern, a little realm all its own. What might be considered his one really ugly act, wounding the corpse of Hotspur in order to get the credit for defeating him, is, for those who do not revere corpses, only a wound to a corpse. Most of all, his salvation for himself and for the audience is that he is screamingly funny. And, although there is much slapstick in him, the humor does not stop at that but touches on the great themes traditional to comic liberation—the gods, the city, and the family. He is a criminal not only because his uncontrolled tastes lead him in that direction, but also because he is a critic of the conventions.

This is perhaps enough to explain the shrewd Hal's attraction to Falstaff. From his earliest youth Hal seems to have known that the official versions of what is good and evil, noble and base, are defective and can hamper political activity. He was one of those who know that success will bring with it a reputation for morality, or that the benefactor of the people will be held to be the good man, whereas those who follow the rules are burdened in such a way that the possibility of their success is compromised. Hal knows that his reputation is sullied by his associations, but turns the stain to his advantage. He who appears to be a low fellow and proves to be a superior one will have a better reputation for that. The noble Hotspur, the exact opposite of Falstaff, whom both Falstaff and Hal despise, spends his short life doing the works of nobility, and all Hal has to do is kill him; this one deed and all of Hotspur's reputation will accrue to him (Part I, V.iv.70–72). He is a takeover specialist.

Hal may very well have thought that Falstaff, who had gone a long way on nature's road, would be able to teach him about what is to be found along it. It is not sufficient to say that he enjoys the Boar's Head merely because he finds there the low, sensual pleasures. For in doing so he also learns something, that those pleasures are real pleasures though unavailable and frowned upon at the court. Nor is it sufficient to say he is there to find out about the lower orders, as he does in playing around rather cruelly with the tapster, Francis (Part I, II.iv.1–109). This would require very little of his time and less of his participation in the low deeds of the place. It is Falstaff who interests Hal there. Falstaff is of the place but expresses it with a spirituality that transcends it. He is a reliable guide to the charms of vice. Hal, it appears, finds life at the Boar's Head very enjoyable, but not so enjoyable as ruling, which makes it easy for him to give it up when there is imperious need to do so. Hal knows that he cannot be number one until his father dies, and he does not waste away observing the pieties while waiting. He surely wants to be king, which means that the prospect of his father's death is not an unmixed sorrow. Hal stays within the limits that require him to wait for his father's death before becoming king, but he tests them in thought at the Boar's Head.

Falstaff is the only inhabitant of the Boar's Head who has self-knowledge, and that seems to be irresistibly charming, at least for a time, to Hal. Falstaff's comments like "A plague upon it when thieves cannot be true one to another" (Part I, II.ii.27–28) remind Hal that there is a question whether civil society's morality is very different from that of thieves, only enjoying a better press. Hal, as opposed to Hotspur, seems to have understood politics the way Falstaff does. His only other comment about his motives in this stage of his life is one that is much more revealing than his statements about his improved reputation:

And we understand him [the Dauphin] well,
How he comes o'er us with our wilder days,
Not measuring what use we made of them.[2]

The French are about to find out what he learned in his apparently
misspent youth. One thing he surely knows is that the usual view that
dissipation of body and of mind destroys a man's strength of character is false, at least for men like himself. His bodily lusts are easily
tamed by his political passions and set up no conflict within him,
partly because he has been purged of romantic expectations from sex,
and his intellectual lusts, by no means becoming an end in themselves,
further his capacity to see well.

The Hal-Falstaff couple is in a way a parody of Aristotelian friendship, the union of two souls that appreciate each other and are rather
indifferent to money or vulgar sensual pleasures, just delighting in
each other even though every man loves himself more than anyone
else, each heightened in the mirror of the other's understanding. This
is a parody, but the parody contains some elements of the real thing.
We have in these two a powerful natural connection, although shot
through with tensions that make it doubtful. Hal enjoys Falstaff and
admires him in a certain supramoral way. That the friendship can be
broken off so brutally proves that it is not a true friendship, which is
the most durable of all attachments. Hal, whose side decency forces
us to take against Falstaff, has the upper hand in the relationship and
performs the hard deeds connected with terminating it. This shows
something about politics and the essentially friendless character of
the king, who has no equals and must subordinate the highest things to
raisons d'état.

Falstaff, of course, profits from the association with the heir apparent, who has money and, especially, sufficient influence to protect him
from the full rigor of the law. He jokes about much greater expectations for the future when Hal will be king. But Hal's utility is not
enough to account for the kind of attachment Falstaff expresses. In
part, Falstaff is not really very ambitious. He wants some money, to
stay out of prison, and to be able to influence appointments. He is a
man of the present without extensive plans for the future. His primary
concern is to live beyond the law, while avoiding the consequences of
living in a society where there is law. In order to do so he has had to
become a careful observer and very quick-witted. But just as Hal's at-

tachment to Falstaff cannot be exhausted by the obvious low motives, Falstaff's motives contain something in addition to the obvious benefits of palling around with a man who is to be king. Part of it seems to be the pleasure of seeing a soul and a character he can hope to make like his own. This is a thrill of complicity, the complicity of understandings, which has a charm all of its own, one not always appreciated by vulgar psychologists. He has a sort of erotic attraction to this promising youngster in whom he would like to see himself reproduced. He looks forward to Hal's being king because he expects Hal on the throne to have a spiritual kinship with him. It is not so much the boast "I know the king" as "the king is mine" that moves him.

Falstaff has a touch of nobility in him, and unlike the others in his crowd, he could have made a political career for himself, although he could not seriously aspire to become a king. His failure to do so could be understood as the usual tale of a promising man undone by unbridled passions. But it is equally plausible that he has turned to that life of his, which he so evidently enjoys, because he sees through or beyond the political careers of the nobles. His reflections on the vanity of honor as opposed to the reality of life give some indication of the kind of critique he has made of such aspirations (Part I, V.iii.30–61). And there are many such reflections about men's not being able to be true to themselves. His descriptions of the pleasures are enticing, for example, his W. C. Fields–like praise of drink in response to his encounter with Hal's puritanical brother John (Part II, IV.iii.84–123).

One can see the charm of Falstaff's and Hal's association in the way they relate to each other in the first scenes. The pleasure consists primarily in their dialectical skill, each trying to outwit the other. It is a combat of masters of self-justification and sophistical argumentation. "I deny your major, if you will deny the sheriff" (where mayor of the city and the major premise of the syllogism by which Hal proves him to be a coward are conflated and sheriff is understood to be the subordinate of the mayor) is a perfect example of the exchanges that prove the dignity of speeches for their own sakes for these two men (Part I, II.iv.489). Hal recognizes the truth of Falstaff's assertion that not only is he, Falstaff, the possessor of wit, in all of its senses, but he also communicates it to others. Hal, who is one of those to whom he communicates wit, loves it and is gifted at it. The two elaborate scenes where Hal conspires to embarrass Falstaff, the double robbery at Gadshill, and the serving man's disguise adopted to overhear what Falstaff says about him, really have as their purpose to see how Falstaff will respond to being caught in his lies. And Falstaff gladly obliges and is breathtaking in his agility. There is nothing to say in response to Falstaff's justification that to say bad things about Hal among bad people is appropriate for a friend in order to protect him from the love of the wicked (Part II, II.iv.315–321). Hal delights in seeing not Falstaff's embarrassment but his skill at avoiding it. Things like this are what constitute the core of their love for each other.

Hal and Falstaff are a pair for whom nothing is sacred, at least in speech. They insult each other without any of the elaborate formalisms that characterize the court. Their insults are the courtesies of this world and are more honest than those in use among the nobles. The content of their discourse is from the outset dedicated to legitimizing the thieves, as if, when Hal takes over the law, they will become the true men. This is interlarded with lighthearted blasphemies. Law and religion are the first targets of these free spirits. Perhaps the most shocking game for Hal to play is the one where he asks Falstaff to play his father and then, as Falstaff puts it, deposes him and himself plays his father, the king (Part I, II.iv.371–475). The most sacred constraints of all, those on which the family is based and which are identical to politics in a hereditary monarchy, are themes here for the most radical theoretical and practical questionings. The question of a son's loyalty and duty to his father is tested to its limits in the two *Henry IV* plays, and Hal neatly straddles the issue by behaving and thinking as freely as he wants and then persuading his father that he is a good and true son. Hal lives in the perspective of his father's death and cannot help but come close to the stark question posed, according to John Locke, by the son stymied by his father: "Father, when will you die?"[3] Hal must be the good son in order properly to succeed his father, but what he brings to his rule is something radically different from and opposed to what his father brought to his. Hal shucks off the family pieties and shows something of his political genius by appearing to adopt them in the end. Falstaff probably taught him how to think this way and is certainly the only person with whom he can act it out.

The impious relationship of Hal and Falstaff, and the pious relationship between Hal and his father, pretty much represent the essential tension between philosophy and obedience to the ancestral so central to the life of Socrates. Falstaff is indeed Henry IV's rival. Hal knows that, although Henry IV does not. Falstaff, playing king, catechizes, as would any good father, his adoptive son on his disorderly friends and life. But, as king, he praises Falstaff. He does this in the form of great classical epideictic rhetoric, an art of which he is a master and which he uses at will throughout the plays. Then Hal wishes to take over the role and the imagined throne. The real son of the father epitomizes the father's role by an extreme attack on Falstaff, whom he calls "that villainous abominable misleader of youth" (Part I, II.iv.455–456). This is the complaint of the fathers against Socrates. And this charge, corrupting the youth, is really what brought Socrates down. He is the rival of the fathers in the education of their children, a function that belongs to the fathers in all traditional social orders, orders that are changed by the success of Socrates.

Socrates' questionings of the sons inevitably leads sons to question their fathers. The Hal-Falstaff relationship is not entirely unlike the one between Socrates and Alcibiades. Alcibiades was the young man of great family and unlimited political ambition with whom Socrates spent a certain amount of time and who was certainly influenced by him, although in ways that are difficult to gauge. Alcibiades' political career had an unlimited character unlike that of any other Athenian statesman, or perhaps any statesman ever. He seemed to want to live without the constraints of any law or convention and actually did so, but was brought down by the forces of convention. In order to see Falstaff and Hal as similar to the Socrates-Alcibiades pair, one must look to Xenophon, who lets us see an Alcibiades who ridicules his guardian, Pericles, using Socratic arguments,[4] and a Socrates who appears coarser and more buffoonish than in Plato. Falstaff tries to prove to the Chief Justice that he is younger than the Chief Justice, an argument not unlike Socrates' attempt to prove that he is more beautiful than Critobolus, and is roundly ridiculed for it.[5] The Chief Justice avers that he is "well acquainted with your manner of wrenching the true cause the false way" (Part II, II.i.107—109). This is the ordinary accusation against Socrates, that "he makes the worse argument appear the better."[6] And this is not merely an empty accusation. Both Socrates and Falstaff practice such an art, which gives them freedom from conventional reasonings. And these are not the only reminiscences of Socrates in these plays. The death of Falstaff is akin to Socrates', as described in *Phaedo*,[7] in that his body appears to have grown cold from the feet up. And there is practically a quote from *Gorgias* in *Henry IV, Part I*, IV.ii.79–80, where Falstaff in Hal's camp describes his disposition to battle: "To the latter end of a fray and the beginning of a feast fits a dull fighter and a keen guest."[8] This comes closer to the heart of the real Socrates. Falstaff is not really a coward, and Hal knows it. Poins tells Hal that he will not "Fight longer than he sees reason" (Part I, I.ii.179). Falstaff is not avid of the glory of the battlefield. Life for him is more important than glory. But he often speaks of death, and in ways that indicate he accepts its inevitability. He will not change his life, for example his sexual behavior, in order to preserve it. He wishes to live as long as possible enjoying the real pleasures of food, drink, sex, and wit. A certain stiff piety surrounds the way we look at Socrates that makes it difficult to see the roisterous gaiety in symposia that are part of a shared philosophic liberation. Surely Falstaff is not Socrates, but this is a kind of comic picture of the Socratic life, no more outrageous than Aristophanes' picture of Socrates. It is actually more tender, because Shakespeare, the poet, has more in common with the philosopher than did Aristophanes, who was a spokesman for poetry in the old war between philosophy and poetry. Shakespeare's plays, as we have seen in this survey, are suffused with a love of reason and what Socrates calls a kind of human wisdom.[9] He reproduces here both the exhilaration of philosophical observation of human life and the kinds of relationships among human beings it can form.

Hal himself is as ambiguous as Alcibiades. He seems to have an irrepressible involvement with Falstaff but is unwilling to draw the conclusion from it, that politics is only a game. Alcibiades seems to have been liberated in the same way and to think that philosophy is in some way the highest, but he is unable to give up politics and so he practices a kind of unconventional politics. Hal does not mind Falstaff's walking through the battlefields ridiculing what goes on there. Falstaff even makes a comedy out of Hal's great moment, his defeat of Hotspur. By faking his own death, he gets a funeral oration out of Hal, as did Hotspur, showing up Hal's oratory, which ennobles the fallen who are no longer dangerous. Falstaff fools Hal by resurrecting himself. Hal seems to accept all of this easily and with amazing equanimity; he pursues his wars without the hot indignation that almost always accompanies warriors. He has certainly seen Falstaff's exposés of justice as it is really practiced in the cities of men, as in Falstaff's dealings with Justice Shallow. Hal as king acts with an efficaciousness unencumbered by morality but knows how to borrow the colors of morality. His simple abandonment of his old friend Falstaff, in order to improve his reputation for justice, follows from a teaching he could have learned from Falstaff. He uses the Chief Justice, whom he himself has struck in disrespect, to punish Falstaff. He therefore endorses the rigorous application of the law, which he does not really respect himself. Hal becomes a real Machiavellian king, which means (contrary to the conventional understanding of how a successful student of Machiavelli will appear) that he is reputed to be just, even while fighting unjust but successful wars. Above all, like the Machiavellian king, he appears to be very religious and manipulates the prejudice in favor of religion by using the prelates. But he is also Machiavellian in the sense that he gives up all the sub- or suprapolitical pleasures that he experienced with Falstaff. He proves the usefulness of Falstaff, but his political ambition allows him to suppress the charms of Falstaff. What is interesting and sinister about Hal is the degree to which politics consumes him even though he is the beneficiary of a powerful critique of it. Shakespeare always maintains for himself such joys as are beyond the unerotic necessities of politics. The depiction of Falstaff is his way of inserting such a reminiscence into the grim realities of English politics, as are Autolycus and Pandarus in other contexts, who are supplemented by truly philosophic presences like Ulysses and Prospero.

The relationship between Falstaff and Hal has something in common with the relation of pederasty described by Pausanias in the *Symposium*,[10] where an older man loves a beautiful and promising boy, and trades an education for intercourse. The attractiveness of the youth is given in exchange for the delightful discourses of the man. Hal may ultimately value Falstaff and the wisdom he imparts only for the political advantages gained from them. Hal and Falstaff can hardly be called friends, and certainly Hal is not a real friend, capable as he is of cutting Falstaff off even though Falstaff dies of his rejection. But there is also something Socratic in their relationship. Hal and Falstaff both have independent sex lives, but it is clear that they enjoy each other's company more than that of those with whom they sleep. They are soul mates, and without any touch of solemnity, they prove the possibility of a purely spiritual association, based upon mutual admiration of intellectual gifts, without necessary admixture of anything bodily, or of money, or of power. Those things are present, but they are not the core of the experience. It is, really, an erotic relationship, the attraction based on the potential for shared insight.

Shakespeare's portrayal of this relationship is precisely the opposite of the current attempt to understand human connectedness by what is called male bonding. As human beings we seem separated; it is only as brutes that we can believe in connection. That is a legacy of Konrad Lorenz's studies of animals where he discovered mechanisms of bonding that have bodily need as their ground. We are apparently unable to believe in anything that does not have a biological base. This is all part of the rebellion against reason. Shakespeare shows us an inspiring connection founded on what is available only to man and is highest in man, our reason. The wonderful recognition of a soul that interests us is treated as an experience as powerful as that of two beautiful young people first seeing each other and falling in love. This is a possibility of human connectedness that cannot be called sublimation or anything else derivative from the bodily sexual desires, although it may sometimes have a connection with them. This form of connectedness, shown at the extreme outer horizons Shakespeare presents to his audience, assures us that there is a certain natural community of men not included in the war of all against all or in the artificial community established to end that war and to protect individuals as individuals. For some moments, at least, there can be a community of men based upon common insights into the truth. This is a community not riven by the opposition of bodies and provides a kind of justification of nonillusionary adherence to eroticism. The souls need the conversation with each other and delight in the resulting common and thereby enhanced awareness of the way things are. Selfishness and selflessness become for a moment the same. Hal, of course, is an unsatisfying lover because he is too political to love for long.

CONCLUSION

Shakespeare seems to have said, following Correggio, "I, too, am a painter."[1] He was a kind of Veronese or Titian, painting the vastest tableaux, turning his great mind to those most important moments in the past where one could find the expression of the most interesting human possibilities and trying to learn from them what a fully human or happy life might be. Such knowledge is not available to the man who is a slave to his own time, and it becomes accessible only by study and reflection. There is no inevitable march of history, only possibilities, learned from history about eternal nature, the true source of creation, as Perdita tells us. The survey of the human spirit, which is what Shakespeare's plays taken together are, instructs us in the complex business of knowing what to honor and what to despise, what to love and what to hate. Shakespeare's moment was a great one because all options were open, and one could imagine a future that could be, if not free from the perpetual conflicts that threaten man's happiness, nevertheless the stage on which the richness and fullness of human potential could be acted out. Shakespeare may well have considered himself and the plays, which when all is said and done really are that self, to be the perfect expression of all that a human being can be without the distortions imposed on him by the beliefs of this or that place. Julio Romano is said to surpass nature, but nature incarnated in Hermione surpasses Julio Romano. The movement is from nature to art to nature. But Shakespeare surpasses that nature in giving us his play, which shows that movement. This is not merely paradox, for nature in the classical sense is perfection, and the most perfect human being, not a fancy or a transcendent abstraction, is the perfection of nature. Hence this artist, who puts into his plays all possible human powers and confronts all possible human temptations, can be said to be the perfection of nature. Hence the artist and nature become one.

The Winter's Tale is a survey of Shakespeare's own soul, as a soul can be presented on the stage. In this play winter is used as the simile of old age, and it is a play that is written, if not in Shakespeare's old age, in the light of his anticipations of death. As Prospero tells us at the end of *The Tempest* that his "every third thought will be of the grave," so Shakespeare here may be showing us another third of the thought of the old wise man, thought of love. Mamillius says that sad tales are best for winter (II.i.25), and this play is indeed tinged with melancholy, but it is also an affirmation of a possible beauty of life. This beauty is best acted out in the play by the story of Florizel and Perdita, but their story is more than matched by the vision of the play as a whole. This play is not the expression of an old man's regrets of a lost youth. It is rather the artist's affirmation—a less immediate and less passionate affirmation than that of two lovers who contemplate each other—of the beauty of his contemplation and imitation of nature, nature that is most itself not in mountains and streams but in the microcosm, man. This is a lovely activity that is beyond love, but the experience of lovers and of an artist such as Shakespeare are mirror images of each other. In its own modest way, and without the radical self-regarding of later artists, this play is about the artist and nature under the aspect of mortality.

It may be thought by some that in interpreting these plays I have concentrated too much on the religious question. It is up to the reader to make up his own mind about this after reading the plays and their continuous explicit and implicit reference to religions ancient and modern. *The Winter's Tale* itself provides the most intricate weaving of the Greek gods and Christian practices. The Delphic oracle actually governs the play, but Hermione is a saint. Here Shakespeare's imagination blends the two, but they are kept separate and accurate in those plays that respect verisimilitude and are less revelatory of the poet's own state of soul. Shakespeare wrote prior to the separation of church and state, which, in spite of its manifest advantages, tends to make us forget that all earlier social and political orders were always ultimately governed by the gods and the vision of the good life mandated by their peculiar character. Politics, naturally, according to Aristotle, deals with the comprehensive good for man, and the first claims we encounter about that comprehensive good are made by the religions and their gods, supported by the authority of the state. No serious man could avoid confronting the conflicting claims of conflicting gods. They were all around him, and they constrained him. There can be no doubt that Shakespeare knew about and was influenced by ancient republicanism, and that it influenced his understanding of the medieval Christian monarchy he depicted in *Richard II*. In his histories he reformulated what monarchy ought to be partly on the basis of the real advantages to be found in ancient republicanism. Shakespeare taught us about the different kinds of political community and the relationships of individuals to them. It is impossible to believe that he was not powerfully aware of the different kinds of gods who patronized the different kinds of lives, particularly when one comes to the questions of love and eroticism. The meaning of erotic agitations and longings depends in large measure on the status of the body, and that status is differently appraised in the world of the Olympian gods and that of the biblical one. Shakespeare is compelled in characters as diverse as Cleopatra and Hermione, Angelo and Falstaff, to think thoughts that reflect on the moral teachings of the religious alternatives.

Shakespeare's erotic sensibility and imagination were obviously very far ranging and full of sympathy for many of the ultimately incomplete and imperfect solutions to the problem of what to do with this great force that brings human beings together and separates them, from Falstaff's whoremongering to Hermione's absolute fidelity, with many stops between. Shakespeare was no less addicted to the charms of the erotic union of two people than are we, nor was he less aware of all that separates us from each other in such relations than are modern artists and thinkers. No one can make us love love as much as Shakespeare, and no one can make us despair of it as effectively as he does. The difference, as I suggested in the beginning of this meditation on some of his plays, between him and us is that he does not assume on the basis of some philosophy that either separateness or union is the fundamental natural given from which the opposite has to be derived. He remains faithful to the phenomena, and shows us erotic connections along with their fault lines. He surely shows us that there is some element in man that is connected with other human beings and that his erotic inclinations lead him to them. But he shows us powerful motives of individuation—not only the obvious, defective

motives such as self-preservation and desire for money, but the incapacity of a single individual to contain all that is beautiful, and the iso-
lating effects of reason, which is not shared by lovers but which points
to another kind of human connectedness, the common perception of
the truth. In Shakespeare man remains the ambiguous animal, whose
pleasures and pains are much more determined by his choices than by
the kinds of accidents that afflict other animals. Of one thing we can be
certain: there is a natural perception of and longing for the beautiful
that is simply irreducible and cannot be derived from lower motives,
an awareness that does not necessarily give us much guidance about
the kind of loves we ought to pursue, that does not simplify our lives,
as some might hope, but rather complicates them. Of course this
awareness can be submerged by doctrine and by reasonings as well as
by unfavorable circumstances, but it is a perennial beginning point for
serious engagement with the world, and we need the poets to provide
us with the words for its expression. This may seem unscientific to the
modern mind, a mere fiction made to elevate poetry, but the test of any
assertion about the nature of eros or any other part of man is whether
it can account for what one actually experiences and for what one
imagines. In this critical respect Shakespeare wins hands down
against Freud or his kind, and, it seems to me, outdoes Rousseau and
the Romantic novelists.

Yes, it is Shakespeare's naturalness and love of nature, not an envi-
ronmentalist's love but a humanist's love of nature, that are his most
salient characteristics. He can show us everything and let us sympathize with much without fear of undermining a teaching or a morality.
It is not as some might like to think that Shakespeare is high and contemporary writers low, for Shakespeare is never high-minded. It is
that Shakespeare knows so well that man is a mixture of high and low
and that what is often understood to be low holds the key to what is
highest. Enobarbus tells us this in his description of Cleopatra, in
whom the "vilest things become themselves" in such a way that even
"the holy priests bless her when she is riggish."[2] Shakespeare sees the
natural beauties that are sometimes present within conventions, but
he also blesses nature when it breaks through convention's encrusta-
tions. He certainly teaches us to love decency and is a writer who can
be recommended safely to children, but he is also capable of showing
us that an Autolycus or a Falstaff sees things that the "higher" types do
not. We are so used to flipping through our TV channels, turning from

vulgar sex and violence to PBS, where we find that the higher things are now bloated excrescences without a reality beneath them. But the lower things are also distorted without their relation to these higher ones. The distinction between high and low culture is completely foreign to Shakespeare, whose plays are both. Our current experiences do not attach us to the low; they make us despair of high and low. When an Enobarbus, a lowly soldier, speaks of Cleopatra, we know that he has higher experiences unknown to our fatuous orators. In Shakespeare there is never any speech that is not related to a real experience, and this is what distinguishes him. He never speaks with the clinical sterility of our scientists, nor with the impoverished ugliness of our popular arts. For us he is something of a miracle, for he neither really shocks our morality nor seems to repress our instincts by his morality. It is all there. He provides us incentives to be good without abandoning ourselves.

The result of this latest reading of Shakespeare for me is the renewed conviction that there is nothing I think or feel, whether high or low, that he has not thought or felt, as well as expressed, better than I have. This is a personal affront because one likes to think that one possesses a uniqueness and special worth that no one else can grasp. This is also a collective affront to the prejudice that our age really knows important things especially in matters sexual that give it a special superiority over all other ages. Even our nihilists pride themselves on their incapacity to say that this age is superior, which they think makes them superior. The one thing they are incapable of conceiving is that there is someone decisively superior to them, whom they ought to go study rather than chastise for failing to support their moralities. To our current disrespectful critics, I would only say, echoing my own experience, "Try it, you'll like it." Undeniably of course there are things that have happened to us that Shakespeare could neither imagine nor foresee, and we need, although we have only a small supply of them, writers who can help us to see ourselves in these times. But for the things that are permanent in us, the existence of which is best proved by Shakespeare's effect on those who read him seriously in all ages and countries, one must return over and over again to his plays. Once the immediate charms of the present are overcome one realizes that our dignity or lack of it comes from the way we confront that which is always in man. In thumbing through the various commentaries on Shakespeare's plays, which are mostly written by mediocre persons, I became aware that they were elevated by their roles as intermediaries between Shakespeare and us. Without necessarily being able to explain it, their reverence for him gave them a vocation in life that contributed to the continuing vitality of his works. A community of the mind is constituted by this great artist and the traditional interpretation that agglomerates around him. This is the closest thing there really is to a "great chain of being." His great soul informs their smaller ones, and thus elevates them, giving them a better *raison d'être* than they would have had had they struck out on their own. Such a tradition leads us back not to some obscure personal "roots," but to Shakespeare. It in no way incapacitates later great artists such as Goethe, who can look out over the valleys of obscure interpreters and face the challenge of the peak, Shakespeare himself. These interpreters cover Shakespeare with much dust, but they do not bury him by neglect. We can always dust him off, as did such a great man as Lessing, much to the chagrin of the English nationalists. It is this tradition of interpretation, not "creative misunderstandings," not empty rebellions against the "agony of influence," but submissive interpretation and delight at the opportunity to associate with one's betters that constitutes civilization for us. Shakespeare animates worlds and armies of men. The abandonment of the great network of interpretation is the abandonment of what was most important for the Duke of Vienna and for Shakespeare: quest for self-knowledge.

NOTES

Chapter One: Romeo and Juliet

1. Niccolò Machiavelli, *The Prince,* chapter 17.

2. Homer, *Odyssey,* book 11, lines 489–91.

3. Plato, *Republic,* 604e; *The Republic of Plato,* trans. with notes and interpretive essay by Allan Bloom (New York: Basic Books, 1968), pp. 430–32; Jean-Jacques Rousseau, *Letter to M. d'Alembert,* chapters 2 and 5.

4. Aristotle, *Metaphysics,* 982b11–19.

5. *The Tempest,* ed. Frank Kermode, Arden Edition (1954; rpt. London: Routledge, 1988), V.i.310–11.

6. Eric Partridge, *Shakespeare's Bawdy* (London: Routledge, 1947), p. 379.

7. Aristotle, *Politics,* 1327b40–1328a1.

8. Alexis de Tocqueville, *The Old Régime and the Revolution,* part 3, chapter 5.

9. Leo Strauss, "The Problem of Socrates: Five Lectures," in *The Rebirth of Classical Political Rationalism: An Introduction to the Thought of Leo Strauss,* ed. Thomas L. Pangle (Chicago: University of Chicago Press, 1989), p. 107.

10. Rousseau, *Emile,* trans. by Allan Bloom (New York: Basic Books, 1979), p. 324; *Social Contract,* book 4, chapter 7, Rousseau's second note; Johann Wolfgang von Goethe, *Wilhelm Meister's Apprenticeship,* book 5, chapter 16; letter to Schiller, 14 March 1798.

Chapter Two: Antony and Cleopatra

1. Plato, *Phaedrus,* 253d–254a.

2. Homer, *Iliad,* book 3, lines 31–56; book 6, lines 281–334; book 13, lines 765–75.

3. Plutarch, *Comparison of Demetrius and Antony,* chapter 3.

4. Thomas Hobbes, *Leviathan*, part 1, chapter 10.

5. Gotthold Ephraim Lessing, *Laocoön*, chapters 20–22.

6. *King Richard II*, ed. Peter Ure, Arden Edition (1956; rpt. London: Routledge, 1988), V.iv, V.vi.30–52.

7. Plutarch, *Life of Antony*, chapters 36 and 67; Plato, *Phaedrus*, 253e–254a.

8. These are the novels, along with Rousseau's *La Nouvelle Héloïse*, discussed in Allan Bloom, *Love and Friendship* (New York: Simon and Schuster, 1993).

9. Edward Gibbon, *The Decline and Fall of the Roman Empire* (New York: Random House, The Modern Library, n.d.), chapter 2, p. 52.

10. Winston Churchill, *Marlborough: His Life and Times* (New York: Charles Scribner's Sons, 1933), vol. 1, p. 40.

Chapter Three: Measure for Measure

1. Montesquieu, *The Spirit of the Laws*, part 4, book 24, chapter 25; part 3, book 14, chapter 11.

2. Machiavelli, *The Prince*, chapter 7.

3. *King Henry IV, Part II*, ed. A. R. Humphreys, Arden Edition (1966; rpt. London: Routledge, 1988), V.v.69–95.

4. Friedrich Nietzsche, *Beyond Good and Evil*, aphorism 168.

5. Lessing, *Laocoön*, chapter 1.

6. Allan Bloom (with Harry V. Jaffa), *Shakespeare's Politics* (Chicago: University of Chicago Press, Midway reprint, 1986), pp. 101–103.

7. Plato, *Republic*, 338c–339a.

Chapter Four: Troilus and Cressida

1. Plato, *Republic*, 388a–391c.

2. Herodotus, *The History*, book 1, chapters 3–5.

3. Machiavelli, *The Prince*, chapter 25.

4. *King Richard II*, III.ii.1–62.

5. Thucydides, *The Peloponnesian War*, book 1, chapter 20; book 6, chapters 53–59.

6. Aristotle, *Poetics*, 1448a–1449a.

7. Rousseau, *Letter to M. d'Alembert*, chapter 7, p. 71, note.

8. Plato, *Apology of Socrates*, 28b–d.

9. Plato, *Alcibiades I*, 132c–133e.

10. Aristotle, *Nicomachean Ethics*, 1123b27–1124a20.

11. Machiavelli, *The Prince*, chapter 9.

12. Pierre Bayle, "Hélène," remark G, *Dictionnaire historique et critique,* 4th edition (Leiden: Samuel Luchtmans, 1730), vol. 2, p. 703.

13. *King Richard II,* I.iii.

14. Plato, *Republic,* 388a–391c.

15. *King Henry IV, Part I,* ed. A. R. Humphreys, Arden Edition (1960; rpt. London: Routledge, 1988), V.iv.70–72.

Chapter Five: The Winter's Tale

1. Cf. Bloom, *Shakespeare's Politics,* pp. 36–38, 51–54.

2. Homer, *Odyssey,* book 24, lines 234–35.

3. Rousseau, *Emile,* p. 400.

4. Herman Melville, *The Confidence Man,* chapter 21.

5. *King Richard II,* III.iv.24–91.

6. *Cymbeline,* ed. J. M. Nosworthy, Arden Edition (1955; rpt. London: Routledge, 1988), II.iv.167–69, 184–85.

7. Aristotle, *Politics,* 1262a21–24.

8. *Cymbeline,* III.vii.41–68.

9. Cymbeline became king in 33 B.C. and reigned for thirty-five years.

Chapter Six: Hal and Falstaff

1. See Machiavelli, *The Prince,* chapters 14 and 17; *The Discourses,* book 2, chapter 13; book 3, chapters 20, 22, 29.

2. Shakespeare, *King Henry V,* ed. J. H. Walter, Arden Edition (1954; rpt. London: Routledge, 1990), I.ii.265–67.

3. John Locke, *Some Thoughts Concerning Education,* sec. 40.

4. Xenophon, *Memorabilia,* book 1, chapter 2, sections 40–48.

5. Xenophon, *Symposium,* book 5, sections 1–10.

6. Plato, *Apology of Socrates,* 19b–c, 23d.

7. Plato, *Phaedo,* 118.

8. Plato, *Gorgias,* 447a.

9. Plato, *Apology of Socrates,* 20d.

10. Plato, *Symposium,* 181c–185a.

Conclusion

1. Words attributed to the Italian painter Correggio on seeing Raphael's *St. Cecilia;* cf. Montesquieu, *Spirit of the Laws,* preface.

2. *Antony and Cleopatra,* II.ii.238–40.

INDEX